UPSETTING COMPOSITION COMMONPLACES

UPSETTING COMPOSITION COMMONPLACES

IAN BARNARD

UTAH STATE UNIVERSITY PRESS
Logan

© 2014 by the University Press of Colorado
Published by Utah State University Press
An imprint of University Press of Colorado
5589 Arapahoe Avenue, Suite 206C
Boulder, Colorado 80303

 The University Press of Colorado is a proud member of
The Association of American University Presses.

The University Press of Colorado is a cooperative publishing enterprise supported, in part, by Adams State University, Colorado State University, Fort Lewis College, Metropolitan State University of Denver, Regis University, University of Colorado, University of Northern Colorado, Utah State University, and Western State Colorado University.

The paper used in this publication meets the minimum requirements of the American National Standard for Information Sciences—Permanence of Paper for Printed Library Materials. ANSI Z39.48–1992

ISBN: 978-0-87421-946-3 (paper)
ISBN: 978-0-87421-947-0 (ebook)

Library of Congress Cataloging-in-Publication Data
Barnard, Ian, 1960–
  Upsetting composition commonplaces / Ian Barnard.
    pages cm
Includes bibliographical references and index.
  ISBN 978-0-87421-946-3 (pbk.) — ISBN 978-0-87421-947-0 (ebook)
  1. English language—Rhetoric—Study and teaching (Higher) 2. English language—Composition and exercises. I. Title.
PE1404.B28 2014
808'.0420711—dc23
                        2013041215

Cover illustration: © PlusONE/Shutterstock

*To my amazing students at California State University,
Northridge, from whom I learnt something every day.*

CONTENTS

ACKNOWLEDGMENTS

I am deeply grateful to the following friends and colleagues, who have (sometimes unwittingly) pointed me toward resources that were essential to this project, and who gave invaluable feedback on earlier incarnations of portions of the text: Jada Augustine, Pamela Bourgeois, Robert Brooke, Irene Clark, Kristin Cornelius, Roxana Dapper, Diane Davis, Anthony Dawahare, Corri Ditch, Karmen Garabekyan, Richard C. Gebhardt, Angela M. Gonzalez, Mary Griffith, Andrea Hernandez, Sharon Klein, Noreen Lace, Carrie Leverenz, Mandy Macklin, Nareen Manoukian, Aneil Rallin, Ronit Sarig, Ryan Skinnell, Joseph T. Thomas, Jr., Sherry Truffin, Tiffany Wampler, Beth Wightman, and Kathleen Yancey.

Thanks, too, to my composition colleagues at California State University, Northridge (CSUN), for so willingly responding to my chapter 3 survey; to the students in my Fall 2011 Approaches to University Writing class at CSUN, for their insights and conscientiousness, and for so generously granting me permission to share their work in chapter 4; and to Elizabeth Burkholder, Kelly Fitzgerald, and the two student writers who requested to remain anonymous, for giving me permission to quote their unpublished work in chapter 5.

The two anonymous reviewers for Utah State University Press helped me to rethink and refine the manuscript with their informed and generous feedback. And I am forever grateful to Michael Spooner, my editor at Utah State University Press, for his enthusiastic and insightful response to this project, as well as Laura Furney, Karli Fish, Daniel Pratt, Beth Svinarich, Nina Moon Ahn, and Kellyn Neumann for their work on this book.

I also thank CSUN, for the sabbatical leave and the College of Humanities Faculty Fellowship that supported my work on this book, as well as Wilkinson College, Chapman University, for a reduced teaching load and research funds that allowed me to complete the book.

An earlier version of chapter 2 was published in *College Composition and Communication* 61.3. A previous version of chapter 3 was published in *Composition Forum* 24. Chapter 5 appeared in *Composition Studies* 34.1, in a significantly different incarnation. And small portions of chapter 6 previously appeared in *symplokē* 13.1–2 and *Reflections: A Journal of Public Rhetoric, Civic Writing, and Service Learning* 7.3. My thanks to the editors and publishers of these journals, for supporting my work and granting permission for portions of that work to be reprinted here. I also thank the journals' peer reviewers, for their careful and sympathetic readings, as well as their revision suggestions for some of the material presented here.

I want to acknowledge the many scholars I have cited throughout this book. They have inspired, influenced, and directed me toward other sources and unexpected directions in ways I can hardly trace anymore. Although it's not customary for the authors of academic publications to mention specific scholars who have had a particular influence on their style or form, I do want to acknowledge Bruce Horner, whose *Terms of Work for Composition* influenced the format and chapter titles of this book, and the late Eve Kosofsky Sedgwick, whose prose and tone (especially in *Tendencies* and *Epistemology of the Closet*)—in addition to her brilliant ideas—continue to inspire and delight me as a writer.

My special thanks and love to Aneil Rallin, for consistently egging me on to complete this project.

UPSETTING COMPOSITION
COMMONPLACES

1

INTRODUCTION
For Theory's Sake

I. DISJUNCTIVE IMPETUSES

Many of the ongoing difficulties teachers face revolve around the "translation" of disciplinary knowledge—especially critical theory—into pedagogical praxis. It often seems that our teaching lags behind our theoretical knowledge by about two decades, and sometimes we wonder if it will ever catch up. This sense of disjunction has been compounded by the difficulty of "teaching" postmodern understandings of subjectivity, truth, and epistemology in increasingly commodified teaching contexts, where consumers expect to purchase clear, identifiable, and literally usable products, and where "knowledge" often means easily digestible and repeatable content rather than analytic skills, critical understandings, or complex world views. Prescriptive "standards," standardized testing, common syllabi, assessments, and outcomes become more important than ideas and dispositions.

Given the growing lag between theory and pedagogy, I am no longer surprised when the law students in my college composition classes believe that good judges are impartial judges, or when the journalism majors insist that effective journalists are objective, despite the fact that both the possibility and desirability of objectivity have been thoroughly discredited in recent and ongoing work in critical anthropology, critical legal studies, postcolonial theory, feminist theory, queer theory, and other fields and disciplines. Either my students' learning in their law, journalism, or other classes is out of sync with cutting-edge scholarship in the disciplines, or their learning is not yet able to withstand the more powerful forces of students' own and societal preassumptions.

DOI: 10.7330/9780874219470.c001

This is not to say that writing instructors have been able to avoid theory-practice disjunctions. The order of business in many composition classrooms and textbooks seems to be business as usual. Despite the assaults on ethnographic disciplines and practices that have taken place for almost four decades now, ethnography-focused writing assignments continue unabated in many composition classrooms. And despite the force of postmodern composition theory—which has persuasively critiqued ubiquitous composition practices and notions like "freewriting" and "authentic voice"—there seems to be little let-up in admonitions to "freewrite" or appeals for "authentic voice" in composition classrooms.

These holdovers are not innocent, and have drawn fire as symptoms of composition's intransigence and conservatism. In 1986, Mas'ud Zavarzadeh and Donald Morton denounced first-year composition as the "last bastion of defense of traditional humanism against radical postmodern critical theory" (Zavarzadeh and Morton 1986–87, 13). Five years later, Lester Faigley, after having cited Zavarzadeh and Morton's acerbic observation, asked, "[I]f we have indeed entered the era of postmodernity, then why has there been so little change evident in the classroom conditions for teaching college writing?" (Faigley 1992, 165). My goals in writing this book were, in part, to find out if Zavarzadeh and Morton's diagnosis still holds true twenty-five plus years later, and, if so, to attempt some answers to Faigley's question.

Faigley noted the disjunctions between composition and postmodern theory, but also pointed to changes in composition that appeared to begin to address postmodern challenges to traditional humanism, and the theories, practices, and pedagogies of composition that aligned themselves with it. However, *Upsetting Composition Commonplaces* delivers the discouraging (though unsurprising) news that, twenty years after Faigley published his book, things haven't changed that much. Hence, I use "upsetting" in my title in both senses of the word, to underscore the force of the discouraging news and urge along the much-needed revolution, as well as to signal my aim of doing some upsetting with this book. Each of the following six chapters addresses one of six formative composition commonplaces: clarity, intent, voice, ethnography, audience, and objectivity. In each case, I have chosen a belief (system) and the practices it animates that inform common, often taken-for-granted or taken-as-axiomatic, understandings in composition and the undergirdings of composition pedagogy. And in each case I attempt to upset the commonplace by demonstrating its incoherence, whether in the context of its explicit or implicit execution of values and assumptions that have been discredited by poststructuralist theory[1], or in its incompatibility with the stated goals of composition studies itself. I also try to account for these disjunctions and offer alternative epistemologies for composition theory and pedagogy that are more theoretically informed and consistent.

These alternatives are not meant to serve as prescriptive correctives, but rather to open up the possibilities of composition. In the introduction to his evocative readings of Derrida, Michael Naas reminds us of Derrida's influence:

> And yes, each time we receive the tradition, each time we take it on, we are offered a chance to receive something unforesee-able and unprecedented within it. Although all our thinking, all our receptions, are illuminated in advance by the horizon of our tradition, our turning toward that horizon is not. Each day we turn toward the sun blindly: with each reading we receive the tradition anew and so are given the chance of encountering something that escapes the simple duality of "taking on the tra-dition"—the simple opposition between accepting or rejecting a tradition as our own. With each reception comes the possibility of rethinking what is our own by receiving it before either we or it have been wholly constituted. For although there may indeed be nothing new under the sun, there is no tradition, no sun even, before we have received it. (Naas 2003, xviii)

I use Naas's admonition to remind my own readers and myself that forms are formative, but not inevitable. I am interested in upsetting the sense of inevitability that often accompanies the composition commonplaces I play with—an inevitability that has been constructed by history, culture, and disciplinarity (including disciplinary histories and the other places where these meaning makers inflect and mediate one another). Later, Naas adds that Derrida's own work analyzes philosophical traditions "in order to reveal something untraditional within them" (Naas 2003, xx). Naas's formulation speaks to dual attempts to resist binary logic in this book: exploding open composition commonplaces to show the differences they house (e.g., rescuing "audience" from expository reductiveness in chapter 6), and a deconstructive impetus to reveal the incoherences already constituted by these commonplaces (e.g., "clarity" meaning everything but clarity in chapter 2).

The diverse antecedents to my work in this book—both in terms of what I see as the central issues that thematize the disjunctions I have described above, as well as the specific scholars who have prompted my interventions—illustrate consistent concerns across sub-fields and theoretical affiliations in rhetoric and composition. In her essay in *An Introduction to Composition Studies*, Lisa Ede (1991) noted the gaps between theory and practice (and between theory and textbooks) in composition specifically, without going into much detail regarding these gaps. In 1992, Faigley gave a summary of the poststructuralist critique of enlightenment conceptions of subjectivity in *Fragments of Rationality* (chapter 4)—I will not recapitulate this well-known critique here, but I do briefly discuss some of the attendant motifs of *Upsetting Composition Commonplaces* in section II below. Faigley's introduction and first chapter provided an overview of the (lack of) impact of postmodern theory and postmodernity on composition studies. A few years later, John Schilb's *Between the Lines* traced the divergences between composition and literary theory, in particular, noting the differing views of subjectivity, language, and rhetoric in the two fields (Schilb 1996, especially chapter 2). Other scholars who have propelled my own work—primarily in their commentary on the relationship between poststructuralism (in some cases, deconstruction) and composition, on the disjunctions between critical theory and composition, and between composition theory and pedagogy—include Linda Brodkey (1996), Sharon Crowley

(1987, 1994), Min-Zhan Lu (1994), Jasper Neel (1988), Louise Wetherbee Phelps (1988), Brooke Rollins (2006), Raúl Sánchez (2005), and Kurt Spellmeyer (1993). *Upsetting Composition Commonplaces* builds on the work begun by these and other rhetoric and composition scholars by filling out their hunches, using some of their questions as starting points for further investigation, attempting to ask new questions, and using their frameworks to examine some of the composition commonplaces that they don't discuss.

The editors of the recent anthology *Beyond Postprocess* hint at the change in nuance that characterizes composition in the twenty-first century in their invocation of "the once sacrosanct gravitational pull of the writing subject" (Dobrin, Rice, and Vastola 2011b, 2). *Once* is the operative word here, pointing to the fact that, albeit quite late in the game, composition can no longer uncritically vaunt discredited humanist constructions of authorship and subjectivity as originating in a unified and autonomous writer. In contrast, gravity and the sacred do not lose their pull overnight; the pull is still there, even though it may no longer be sacrosanct (or gravitational). However, the loss of its power might mean the interrogations can finally be heard, and that the time is now ripe for some of these composition commonplaces to be upset. It is time for new questions to be asked, and new models of composing, teaching, and theorizing to be developed on the heels of these questions. As the *Beyond Postprocess* editors put it, "In defiance of the commonsensical recognition we may finally ask: Who or what is the subject of writing? What would it mean to understand the subject of writing as strictly textual? How is identity constructed and circulated in writing environments and postmodern writing practices?" (3). These are some of the additional questions that animate my critique of composition "commonplaces" in the following chapters, and which also indicate the continued resilience of discredited conceptualizations of subjectivity and indefensible epistemologies of composing.

The white elephant on the page here is theory itself, the resistance to theory in general, and the resistance to theory in composition, specifically among compositionists (scholars and teachers).[2] Kory Ching (2007) has, in fact, argued that anxiety over theory in composition can be attributed to theory's throwing of cherished composition commonplaces into question. I address the possible ideological stakes in antagonism toward theory—and the ways in which attacks on theory can serve as a cover for other projects—in chapter 2, but I want to briefly riff on Ching's tantalizing point here. Even an unconscious recognition of how the work of theory might undermine common pedagogical practices in composition, as well as the rationales for these practices (and for composition programs and policies as a whole), might instigate backlashes against theory, in addition to the more common fears of and attacks on theory as elitist, inaccessible, and irrelevant. The resistance to theory can also take the form of composition's pedagogical imperative, which I discuss in section IV below. While the insistence that work in composition studies should properly be about teaching can appear to operationalize (and frequently is presented as doing so) a concern for students—and translate composition's social justice disposition into action—it can mask 1) ideological and material antagonism to the arguments of theory, 2) anti-intellectualism (which itself can metonymize political distaste for theory), 3) a reluctance to interrogate and modify/upset one's own pedagogy, and 4) stasis and a resistance to change in general (whether for reasons of arrogance, familiarity, comfort, fear, overwork, or the appalling politics and materialities of contingent academic labor in the United States). If anything, these deferrals and displacements point to the urgency of working through theory and making apparent the often subterranean theoretical impasses in the teaching of composition.

II. COMMON THREADS

Several themes cut across the following chapters, and hence suture together the specific topics I address in *Upsetting Composition Commonplaces*. I highlight some of their foundations here, in order to avoid unnecessary repetition in chapters 2–7, to lay ground for my critiques of composition theory and pedagogy in twenty-first century US, and for my own theoretical, political, compositional, and pedagogical affiliations in this book.

Axiom 1: The Humanist Subject Is Dead

In 1990, Andrea Lunsford and Lisa Ede predicted that "the challenge of responding to contemporary critiques of the author and of the subject comprises one of the most important tasks faced by those in composition in the coming years" (Lunsford and Ede 1990, 140). Although poststructuralism announced the death knell of the humanist subject, composition—for various reasons and in multifold incarnations that I will attempt to unpack in the following chapters—has been reluctant to let go. Lunsford and Ede's yoking together of the concepts of author and subject hints at composition's particular entanglement in the modernist self, given the difficulty of denying subjectivity to the living authors to which composition attends most closely—students in the classroom. And, as Jeff Rice (2005) suggests, expressivism and process pedagogy are attached to the modernist subject.

In the United States, composition's historical ties to social justice movements—and, in particular, activism for educational equity—linked the idea of process to ideas of individualism, upliftment, and agency that belied poststructuralism's more complicated postulations of subjectivity. However, composition's balking at the evaporation of the liberal subject and its loyalty to romantic myths of the self-contained author also evince a refusal to recognize subjectivity's social constitution and imbrications. As Bruce Horner suggests, "recognizing the social production of consciousness meets with resistance because it undermines the concept of the Author as a quintessentially autonomous individual on which English literary study specifically but also academic institutions and capitalist ideology generally depend" (Horner 2000, 217). I would argue that this is a fortiori the case for composition, as my explorations around intent and voice in chapters 3 and 4 demonstrate. But bourgeois constructions of subjectivity are also intricated in the assumptions about objectivity that I interrogate in chapters 5 (Ethnography) and 7 (Objectivity), since a belief in the self-contained subject is a precursor to the conviction that the subject can get beyond or outside itself, a conviction that undergirds faith in the possibility and desirability of objectivity.[3]

Axiom 2: The Author Is Dead

See axiom 1. Also, cherished romantic constructions of the unitary, solitary author who is the sole originator of His writing have been displaced by the recognition of the culturally and historically contingent nature of authorship, especially in relation to ideologies of individualism and their emergence in bourgeois capitalism. The belief in the Author as sole originator of meaning belies poststructuralism's claims to language's determinations (and unpredictabilities), and to the social and political contexts that shape authorship and writing. What is composition's twenty-first century relationship to what Susan Miller (1989, 3) called "the now easily deniable claptrap of inspired, unitary 'authorship' that contemporary theorists in other fields have so thoroughly deconstructed"?

The romantic visions of authorship persist in composition, as I discuss in chapter 3, despite composition's own investments in process, collaboration, and, now, technology, that seem—notwithstanding Rice (2005) in axiom 1 above—to run starkly counter to Romantic/romantic and modernist constructions of authorship. For poststructuralist theory, assumptions of authenticity—whether in reference to voices, texts, processes of writing, or writing subjects—are constructions that belie the non-self-subsistence of the non-foundational, decentered, and radically contingent subject, a subject that composition studies has often been reticent to embrace. As Faigley pointed out in *Fragments of Rationality*, composition studies has proven least receptive to postmodern theory in its refusal to surrender its belief in the writer as an autonomous self, even at a time when extensive group collaboration is practiced in many writing class-rooms. Since the beginning of composition teaching in the late nineteenth century, college writing teachers have been heavily invested in the stability of the self and the attendant beliefs that writing can be a means of self-discovery and intellectual self-realization. (Faigley 1992, 15)

Faigley's observations here are important on several counts. Not only does he identify a problematic composition precept, but the internal contradiction he describes in the first sentence quoted above also illustrates a field that is already at odds with itself, in addition to being out of step with postmodern theory. Faigley gestures toward the longevity and resilience of compo-sition's outmoded values and assumptions, both in terms of their historical continuity and in the ways in which they inform, define, and even constitute the discipline. The beliefs that these values and assumptions inform and animate erupt all over com-position, from processes like "freewriting" to personal narrative assignments to specialist and institutional rationales for compo-sition courses and programs.

Axiom 3: Writing Is Writing

Postmodernism blurred previously taken-for-granted distinc-tions between high and low art, while deconstruction enabled the destabilization of all binaries, as well as the demonstration of the arbitrary and ideological formations that constitute(d) these binaries in the first place. I include binaries like creative/expository, fiction/nonfiction, literature/composition, and stu-dent/writer in this compass, all of which hold formative sig-nificance for composition studies, and whose parameters reso-nate from the high art/low art opposition. Distinctions between "literature" and nonfiction writing, in fact, are becoming ever more solidified as composition seeks to assert its distinctive-ness and influence (especially in high school curricula, as I discuss in several of the following chapters in relation to California's Expository Reading and Writing Course for high school students), even as these distinctions become more difficult to defend and sustain outside of composition.[4] William Covino and Gary Olson both articulate axiom 3 pointedly for my purposes, each indicating a different set of consequences—both equally important—that should flow from it. Covino, commenting on postmodern literary theory and the breakdown of the category Literature, reminds us, "All texts being equal, so to speak, any genre—a freshman essay, lyric poem, casual conversation, scientific treatise, lab report—is legitimate game for the critic, and each is potentially rich in 'symbolic action'" (Covino 1988a, 121). Covino's reminder seems to align with composition's attention to and legitimation of student writing as classroom text, text to be studied, and text to be worked on. However, as I explain in my discussions of clarity (chapter 2) and intent (chapter 3), we often don't treat students' texts the same way we treat professional writing in the composition classroom, especially writing categorized as "Literature." We also often make unfounded distinctions between "creative" and "expository" writing that are more about preserving composition's place than enabling student writers. Olson, in a review of Stanley Fish's *How to Write a Sentence, and How to Read One*, concludes, "One effect of this book—and I believe it is intentional—is that through its performance it demonstrates the importance of not separating literary analysis from the teaching (and learning) of composition; discourse productions and discourse reception are two sides of the same coin" (Olson 2012, 446). My discussions of clarity, intent, and objectivity (chapter 7) also highlight the unconscious and explicit distinctions we often make between fiction and nonfiction texts—both in the field of composition and in the composition classroom—in terms of a disjunction between reception and production, between how and what we read versus how and what we teach (tell) students to write, and the ways in which these distinctions shore up composition's humanist investments. The chapters that follow repeatedly note the uncritical recuperation of questionable distinctions between different types of texts in composition studies and teaching, as well as my view of the unfortunate effects of this recuperation for student writing, students as writers, and for composition as a field of inquiry.

Axiom 4: Students Are Writers

Following my above interrogation of the student/writer binary, and notwithstanding axiom 2, this book affirms composition's breakthrough insistence that student writers are authors—or, as the popular composition textbook title puts it, "Everyone's an Author" (Lunsford, Ede, Moss, et al. 2013)—and that this recognition is important and has consequences.[5] However, I also chronicle the many ways in which composition fails to fulfill the promise of this axiom: it often resorts to an implicit reliance on hegemonic hierarchies that deauthorize student writers by distinguishing students from "real writers" and student texts from the published work of professionals. This is especially apparent in the invocation of clarity (chapter 2) and intent (chapter 3) in composition, usually with reference to students and student texts. I also address this inconsistency in the context of composition scholars' use and citation of student work (chapter 5), and the kinds of writing students are encouraged to read but not emulate in their own work (chapter 6). Min-Zhan Lu's devastating characterization of English studies as "a discipline which, on the one hand, has often proclaimed its concern to profess multiculturalism but, on the other hand, has done little to combat the ghettoization of two of its own cultures, namely composition teaching and student writing" (Lu 1994, 442) points to the political implications and consequences of composition's failure in this arena—the "ghettoization of student writing" denigrates the authority of student experience, denies students the right to their own language (chapter 7), and makes a mockery of our pretentions to enact critically conscious and social justice-oriented pedagogies in composition.[6]

By now it should be apparent that, not only do the above axioms overlap and intersect, but there are also important hypertextual epistemologies at work in this book. These categories, and the frames that demarcate them from one another, are somewhat arbitrary. If writing is writing, then students must be writers. And if the subject is dead, then the author must be as well. The book's chapters, too, bleed into one another. We can only fetishize the (student) author's intent (chapter 3) if we believe in the autonomous composing subject, and humanist constructions of writerly voice so often go hand-in-hand with appeals to authorial intent that it seems intent and voice should interweave, should parallel and overlay one another. In his warning to teachers against co-opting student texts, Brooke Horvath suggests a relationship between intent and the problem of voice that I treat in chapter 4: "If this happens, students may too readily conclude that success depends not upon fully realizing one's intentions, fully conveying one's meaning, fully expressing one's feelings or actualizing one's voice, but upon aping the teacher" (Horvath 1994, 210). A unique voice becomes an expression of individual intent; in both cases, the liberal subject is unified and seemingly independent of the sociality that shapes it.

The topics I have written about also ripple out into connections with other topics I have not (explicitly) treated. Rebecca Moore Howard, for instance, makes a connection between, on the one hand, punitive and overly broad definitions of plagiarism and, on the other, the denial of students' status as authors:

> If we faculty have difficulty comprehending and manipulating the language of the various academic cultures, how much more difficult a task do undergraduate students face as they are presented with a bewildering array of discourse, none of which resonates with the languages of their homes and secondary schools? How much more difficult is the task when students facing this cacophony are denied one of the basic tools—patchwriting—for sorting through and joining the conversations? If we can begin recognizing our students' work ("even" when it obviously includes patchwriting) as the work of authors, we will be helping them to become more successful authors. (Howard 1999, 137)

More on the borders of this book in section III below.

III. ROADS NOT TAKEN

I do not wish to imply that this book is exhaustive, and, certainly, there are other composition commonplaces and taken-for-granted assumptions in composition studies and pedagogy that seem to be at odds with what we have learned from critical theory, to which I might have devoted additional chapters in this book. I can only gesture toward some of those topics here. For instance, plagiarism, writing, English-only, students (as the subject of composition[7]), and identification (the assumption that students work best when they can "identify" with a reading or writing assignment) were some of the additional possibilities I considered. The first four already have a substantial and impressive body of scholarship devoted to them, and I didn't see the need to replicate that work here, but I do want to briefly point toward some of the tantalizing possibilities of three of these areas of inquiry in terms of upsetting composition commonplaces

Plagiarism

Rebecca Moore Howard (1999), in addition to other scholars, has devoted considerable resources and passion to attacking the demonization of plagiarism in composition pedagogy (and in academia as a whole). She points out how composition's conventional and uncritical representation of plagiarism is at odds, not only with poststructuralist and postmodern understandings of authorship and creativity, but also with the underlying impetus of work in composition that unpacks hypostatized conceptualizations of composing. This does not mean, of course, that these insights have substantially impacted composition classrooms (this is a fortiori the case outside of composition), or even that some of the most progressive teachers' syllabi don't continue to make ritual nods in the direction of moralistic and punitive humanist beliefs about plagiarism. Sean Zwagerman articulates this contradiction in his review of *Pluralizing Plagiarism*: "Poststructuralist thinkers suddenly forget everything they claim to believe about textuality and authorship when the text in question is a student's essay: plagiarism is simply an empirical textual fact indicative of suspect authorial intentions" (Zwagerman 2009, 883).[8] Fortunately, the works of Howard and other intellectual property scholars are slowly making their way into composition textbooks, which are now starting to nuance previously pat admonitions against plagiarism, some of which (Lunsford, Ede, Moss, et al. 2013; Howard 2014) even reference "patchwriting," the term Howard coined to explain the painful process by which student writers gain academic literacy through work with secondary sources.

Writing

The twenty-first century necessity to move our understanding of composition beyond writing has received much attention from scholars working in digital and visual rhetoric and composition (e.g., Blair 2011; Hill and Helmers 2004; Ulmer 2003; Wysocki et al. 2004) and non-alphanumeric scripts that challenge the western rhetorical tradition (e.g., Baca 2008), and may in fact signal significant rethinking and reevaluation of the field itself, not to mention the ways in which hypertext and computer software programs unsettle traditional understandings of "writing" per se. This work, together with the new literacy technologies that have transformed the materiality of writing (both noun and verb) in the past forty years, have probably had a greater impact on the composition classroom than the scholarship around plagiarism, if all the new composition textbooks focusing on images (e.g., Faigley et al. 2004) and the curricula and syllabi moving toward blogging, websites, and e-portfolios are any indication. And the transformation of "writing" also impacts the commonplaces treated in the following chapters—for instance, the poster on "Digital Rhetoric" in the June 2013 issue of *CCC* points out, via James Zappen, that, as the lines between composer and audience blur in digital writing environments, so might collaboration supplant persuasion as the primary rhetorical impetus ("Digital Rhetoric" 2013). This usurpation formatively impacts the constructions of audience that I discuss in chapter 6.

Not surprisingly, there is still plenty of resistance—there are many composition teachers who will not accept digital papers and who grade only on paper—and the possibilities of tokenization and co-optation remind us that composition could continue uninterrupted and minimally changed, but with a fresh veneer and lip-service to fashionable new media. Cynthia Selfe (2009) warns that shifts in the direction of digital composition should not mean merely transferring existing writing assignments onto the web, but radically rethinking what composing means.

English-Only

The more recent critique of composition's "English-only" imperative (e.g., Horner, Lu, and Matsuda 2010; Horner and Trimbur 2002; Trimbur 1999) has come, belatedly, in the wake of postcolonial theory; a more critical interrogation of the field's US-centrism and imperialist collusions; increasing work in and attention to composition in transnational and international contexts; and more pointed interrogations of composition's processes, functions, and effects in a resolutely multilingual United States, as well as in the maelstrom of accelerating globalization in general. Related work on World Englishes (Canagarajah 2009) doesn't so much address English dominance in composition, but rather questions why, if we are composing in English, a prescriptive and monolithic US English should be privileged in US composition classrooms, given the various communities worldwide who now communicate in many varieties of English, some of whom outnumber metropolitan English speakers (not to mention the varieties of Englishes and hybrid languages used in the United States). The latter work certainly seems to complement composition scholarship and activism around "standard English" that has been taking place in the United States for decades now, leading up to—and as a result of—the Conference on College Composition and Communication's Students' Rights to Their Own Language resolution of 1974 (Conference 1974). This work has exposed the lie of the naturalness of academic English—and the other linguistic conventions that are enforced in composition classrooms—and pointed to the privileging and exclusions these conventions produce (e.g., Brodkey 1996; Smitherman 1977; Spellmeyer 1993; Young 2009). But the question of "English-only" in the US composition curriculum doesn't seem to have yet made much impact in actual classrooms. Certainly, at a large, comprehensive public university where I taught for ten years, and where first-year composition courses are dispersed across six departments and programs (only one of which is called "English"), no one yet seems to have thought to ask why students are required to write all their assignments in English, despite the richness of the school's multicultural and multilingual student population. Or, perhaps everyone assumes that English-only is a given. This is another composition commonplace worth upsetting.

The brief discussions above of plagiarism, writing, and English-only provide a sampling of the other areas of inquiry that might connect with the work I undertake in this book. Indeed, many assumptions that inform the above commonplaces also undergird the ones I discuss in the following chapters, and, in some cases, the topics enticingly intersect and productively overlap. For instance, in chapter 7 (Objectivity) I note the ways in which dominant linguistic prescriptions are coded in terms of objectivity, a construction that resonates with my above observations on World Englishes and English-only composition. I hope these intersections also signal how so many precepts of composition are intricated in the theoretical inconsistencies I trace—and how thoroughly this intrication has been affected—and I hope they offer pathways for my readers to use some of the principles of this book in other composition contexts, and in relation to other composition commonplaces. In this sense, the templates I provide should be envisaged as sample embodiments of theoretical arguments that point to the larger picture of composition's incoherence and the other spaces that inhabit it.

IV. THE PEDAGOGICAL IMPERATIVE

I take seriously Karen Kopelson's (2008) caveat against seeing theory as practice, as well as her general admonitions against always and only envisaging theory as something to "apply." In US literary studies, critical theory often gets reduced to a smorgasbord of "schools" that students sample (one school a week) from a prescribed anthology, with the goal of then "applying" one or more to one or more literary texts—the latter being the endpoint and the privileged object of study, of course. Theory, then, doesn't have value in and of itself. Hopefully composition can avoid subjecting theory to this tragic fate.

However, I understand that what I am doing in this book is both similar to and different from the problematic construction of theory articulated so insightfully by Kopelson. I'm not necessarily arguing that we should "apply" poststructuralist theory to/ in the composition classroom, but I am suggesting that we need to think through the implications of poststructuralist theory for pedagogy. In other words, I believe that poststructuralism has radical consequences for composition as a field—including the teaching of composition—and that the consequences of taking poststructuralism seriously could include rethinking many of the field's commonplaces, as well as its raison d'être. Mine is an analytic emphasis, rather than a calculus of "translating" theory into practice.

The pedagogical imperative can be another particularly coercive and ensnaring stick in the field of composition, and has been challenged by many well-regarded compositionists, including Gregory Colomb (2010), Sidney Dobrin (2011), Karen Kopelson (2008), Andrea Lunsford (1991), Gary Olson (1991; 2008), Bronwyn Williams (2010), Lynn Worsham (1991, 2002), and the new "school" of postprocess compositionists who question whether composition studies should even be about pedagogy in the first place (e.g., Dobrin, Rice, and Vastola 2011a).[9] While some of these scholars do not deny the importance of studying student writing and the teaching of writing, they believe that making these subjects the field's only purview is reductive and denies composition's significance in attending to, among other things, writing and other literacies and discourses inside and outside of academia. My insistence on the value of theory also leads me to be skeptical of and resistant to invariably having to apply theory to practice, especially when practice is conflated with teaching. This book is certainly replete with examples of what I see as both progressive and regressive composition teaching practices, and I offer suggestions for possible directions for a poststructuralist composition pedagogy. However, I want to forewarn readers who may be coming to this book in search of detailed syllabi, assignments, and fully developed pedagogical protocols that they are bound to be disappointed. My pedagogical suggestions are meant to be evocative, suggestive, invitational, and hopefully inspirational, but I have left them at the suggestive level precisely because my interest lies more in diagnosing the fault lines of composition's refusal of poststructuralism, rather than in providing "solutions" in the form of teaching templates, and because I want to signify the discussion of theory as interesting and important in its own right. Besides, I have every confidence that my readers will come up with much more inventive and effective poststructuralist composition pedagogical practices than the ones I offer in the pages that follow.

NOTES

1. Although poststructuralism usually refers to the conglomeration of philosophical challenges to humanist epistemologies and conceptualizations of language as referential, and postmodernism to new formations (or, at least, new understandings of old formations) in art and society, I sometimes use these terms interchangeably to reflect my sources' use of the terms, and to signal the ways in which poststructuralist theoretical precepts undergird many postmodern dispositions toward and understandings of art, history, creation, and language, and vice versa.

2. See McLemee (2003) and Olson (2002, 2008) for some accounts of the "theory wars" in composition. See Dobrin (2011) for a discussion of composition's hostility toward theory.

3. For further discussions of the subject in the context of rhetoric and composition, see Miller (1989) and Sánchez (2005). For a critique of the subject from the perspective of posthumanism, see Dobrin (2011, especially chapter 3).

4. For further critique of the fiction/nonfiction distinction, see Lanham (2007, 94–95, 139).

5. For some arguments about constructing composition (and other) students as writers, see Barnard (2002), Brodkey (1996, 203), Elbow (1995), Horner (1997, 2000), Howard (2006), Isaacs and Jackson (2001), Lu (1994), and Miller (1991).

6. See Spellmeyer (1993) for a discussion of the demeaning treatment accorded to student-authored texts in composition classes.

7. See Dobrin (2011) for a discussion of this commonplace and an overview of some of the other scholarship that has addressed this topic.

8. See Rebecca Moore Howard (1999, xxii) for further discussion of the disjunctions between theory and practice regarding plagiarism policies.

9. See Worsham (2002, 102) for an explanation of this dispute in composition studies.

2
CLARITY

My goal in this chapter is to interrogate the concept of "clarity" that has become a discursive sine qua non of effective student writing. The virtues of clarity are routinely expounded or assumed in composition handbooks, rubrics used to evaluate student writing, the everyday informal interactions of writing instructors with their students and with each other, the stated philosophies of many college composition programs in the United States, and the course descriptions and expectations of other college faculty (including faculty who work with graduate students). I take issue with the fact that clarity's virtues are taken for granted by analyzing the ways in which assumptions about clarity's obviousness, objectivity, and innocuousness instead conceal the ideological work that is done in the name of clarity, and by examining composition's ramifications from the values embedded in this insistence on clarity.

I have no doubt that various kinds of writing have their place, and that each has drawbacks and advantages. My primary hope, then, is to neither defend nor excoriate writing that is constructed as "clear" or writing that is demonized as "unclear," nor to rehabilitate "muddy prose" by revealing the precision of its arguments. The former effort would merely reverse the problematic binary that I interrogate here. And, while I do believe that form and content cannot be easily separated, and that form carries ideological resonances, its trajectories are not singular and predetermined, a topic I shall return to in chapter 6. The latter argument (the rehabilitation of "muddy prose") would suggest that clarity can, eventually, be "objectively" determined, a suggestion that runs counter to my analysis of the ways in which appeals to clarity are often deployed (and which

DOI: 10.7330/9780874219470.c002

would be inconsistent with my critique of objectivity in chapter 7). I *am* interested in unpacking the values that appeals to clarity implicitly champion and abjure. I hope to show that clarity, although a composition commonplace, is neither axiomatic nor transparent, and that the clear/unclear binary that informs the positing of clarity as a goal of effective student writing is itself unstable, precisely because of the ideological baggage that undergirds its construction. I make this argument by finding traces of composition's insistence on student writers' clarity in the attacks on the writing styles of critical theorists—attacks that present a resistance to the politics of critical theory as a critique of purple prose.

I. THE REIGN OF CLARITY

A first-year composition course description at an institution where I have recently taught explains that students will develop skill in "expressing ideas clearly," and clarity rears its enigmatic head again in the rubric that all instructors of the course are required to use when scoring student portfolios. This rubric defines a strong thesis as "clear, insightful, and thought-provoking." Rhetoric and composition graduate students in the school's MA program are reminded that the point of their thesis project must be "clearly articulated and supported" in their proposal, and that the project must be "clearly situated within literary or theoretical traditions" (English Department Website 2007). Unsurprisingly, a quick Google search shows that my institution is not unique in this regard: sample online rubrics for writing assignments at Winthrop University, Florida State University, The University of Texas at Austin, and Case Western Reserve University, for instance, all demand that successful student essays exhibit clarity in some form, whether by embodying "a *clear* thesis and organizational strategy," a "*clear* organization and focus," or a "*clear* controlling idea" (my emphasis), or by "clearly" indicating the "direction" of the paper, or developing a "clear" introduction and conclusion ("Building Rubrics" 2009; Franks 2009; Koster 2008; "Sample Grading Rubrics" 2006). An "unclear" one of any of these is penalized. Student writing outside the academy seems to be equally under the spell of clarity: a website sponsored by the Home Educators Association of Virginia provides a "rubric for written composition" where the first criterion under the "main idea/topic sentence" scoring category hinges on whether a student paper's main idea or topic sentence is "unclear" (Munday 2008). It should be noted that many of these rubrics, and others like them, derive from rubrics published in composition textbooks and scholarship, including books used to train composition instructors (e.g., Lippman 2003).

Injunctions for clarity are reiterated self-righteously in writing handbooks, composition textbooks, rubrics, syllabi, classroom talk, and faculty conversations on campuses all over the United States. As Lester Faigley points out, in 1950 the first edition of James M. McCrimmon's popular and repeatedly reissued writing textbook, *Writing With a Purpose*, included a section on clarity (Faigley 1992, 151). In 2008, the companion website for Michael Harvey's 2003 handbook, *The Nuts and Bolts of College Writing*, continues this tradition by proclaiming,

> If there's one writing quality that *Nuts and Bolts* emphasizes more than any other, it's clarity. Being clear in your thoughts and your words—saying what you actually intend to say, and doing it in such a way that your reader understands you—is your highest duty as an expository writer, more important than beauty or elegance or even originality. Without clarity you're not really communicating, just going through the motions. (Harvey 2008)

In all of this deferral to clarity, however, there is no discussion of what clarity means or how one knows if something is clear or not. When invoked, clarity's desirability is almost always taken for granted, and is almost always spoken of as if its meaning were obvious (as if we all know if something is clear, and as if my definition of clear will always be your definition of clear). So what does "clarity" mean? In the next section, I attempt to begin to answer this question by highlighting the telling slippages that occur around discourses of clarity. I do this by examining how the clarity mandate functions in the arena of published expository writing—especially in attacks on critical theory—before returning to the question of student writing in section III.

II. THE RUSE OF CLARITY

We can construct various interlocking histories, antecedents, and trajectories for the current hegemony of clarity as a criterion of effective student writing. In a 1969 *College English* article indicting the composition textbooks he saw as undergirding the teaching of "mechanical," "sterile," and "meaningless" student writing, William E. Coles, Jr. found a paradigm shift from a nineteenth century belief in "the moral fusion of writing as an action with the standards by which that actions is measured" to an obsession with clarity and correctness in textbooks of the 1960s (Coles 1969). Another such history might include Anis Bawarshi's discussion of Locke's claim that the only beneficial province of rhetoric is "order and clearness," and how Locke's 1690 reduction of rhetoric influenced eighteenth- and nineteenth-century conceptualizations of rhetorical invention as a regulative skill rather than a generative art (Bawarshi 2003, 177).[1] Richard Lanham also looks to the history of rhetoric, tracing the origins of clarity as "the dominant prose virtue" to Aristotle's *Rhetoric* (Lanham 1983, 199; 2007, 83), and later arguing that the triumph of clarity signals the rejection of rhetoric, which was always associated with obfuscation and deception (Lanham 2006, 137–40). In this narrative, then, we might say that contemporary composition's concern with clarity is a part of the discipline's continuing attempts to legitimize itself, either by looking back (with questionable accuracy) to a long rhetorical tradition or by distancing itself from history, attempting to overcome the stigma of rhetoric, to mark itself as science rather than artifice.[2]

A different history of clarity might look to Lanham himself, Joseph M. Williams (1981), and others, who popularized the merits of "the plain style" beginning in the 1970s.[3] Lanham's original 1974 *Style: An Anti-Textbook* constituted a plea for composition teachers, courses, and textbooks to focus on style, and begins with a denunciation of the obsession with clarity in composition. Lanham rightly recognized that clarity could mean different things in different contexts, and felt the obsession with it was responsible for everything that was wrong with prose in the United States, in addition to denying the pleasures of language and writing. However, Lanham's work is not without its own inconsistencies (for instance, Lanham offers a scathing lampoon of jargon, only to insist that jargon is "fun") and problematic politics—the denunciation of clarity is presented as a corrective to "Our sentimental mass democracy" that "denies the very idea of standards" (Lanham 2007, 170). And, because Lanham interpreted clarity broadly enough to include seemingly tortured syntax in specific disciplinary and institutional contexts, he saw no inconsistency between his scorn for clarity and his championing of the "plain style" in his later work (an inconsistency that he addresses in the 2007 second edition of *Style*). Lanham's (1987) *Revising Prose* was concerned with, as the author himself put it, "translating the Official Style into plain English" (v), though in Lanham's (2006) *The Economics of Attention*, he conceded that the "C-B-S" (clarity-brevity-sincerity) theory of communication "doesn't always work" (141). He still insisted, however, that "[o]f course we should always get the lard out of our prose. I have written two textbooks and two videos that show how to do this" (142).

In each of these cases, the instantiation or recuperation of clarity has political motives and implications beyond the literal desire to enjoy "clear" writing. Clarity's imbrication in larger social and political discourses is best illustrated in the trajectory that most interests me here, where calls for clarity in student writing intersect with complaints of obfuscation in scholarly writing. With the ascendancy of critical theory in the second half of the twentieth century, charges of willful obscurantism were hurled from anti-intellectuals, from readers who found theory difficult and frustrating, from critics on the Right who felt threatened by the ideologies of postmodernism and poststructuralism, from critics on the Left who believed that theory's density diminished its political efficacy, and from those inhabiting any combination of these positions. Daniel Smith points out that charges of using inflated language to attempt to elevate empty or inadequately explicated ideas are nothing new to the humanities, but that "theory is the target de jour of academic gatekeepers faithfully committed to maintaining standards of 'clarity' and 'rigor'" (Smith 2003, 526). The *Philosophy and Literature* journal famously conferred its "bad writing" award on Judith Butler in 1998,[4] and it is surely no coincidence that the culminating example of exclusionary and inefficient writing in Susan Peck MacDonald's *Professional Academic Writing in the Humanities and Social Sciences* is Fredric Jameson, a familiar target in attacks on difficult writing (MacDonald 1994, 193–95). Tellingly, MacDonald's supposedly scientific analysis of Jameson's prose never addresses the substance of Jameson's ideas, focusing instead on syntactic length, nominalization, and nonconcrete verbs. By bracketing content, MacDonald not only avoids dealing with the implications of Jameson's argument, but also suggests that style is completely independent of meaning— as if certain ideas aren't expressed more effectively in specific styles, but instead there is one generic and universal style that is always best.

David Orr's (1999) *Journal of Cnservation Biology* article, "Verbicide," makes the ideological implications of an argument about prose style more explicit. It begins as an attack on young people's apparently diminishing vocabularies due to technology. Orr then accuses some academics of colluding in this decline:

> However manifested, our linguistic decline is aided and abetted by academics, including whole departments specializing in various forms of postmodernism and the deconstruction of one thing or another. They have propounded the idea that everything is relative, hence largely inconsequential, and that the use of language is primarily an exercise in power, hence to be devalued. They have taught, in other words, a pseudo-intellectual contempt for clarity, careful argument, and felicitous expression. Being scholars of their word they also write without clarity, argument, and felicity. Remove the arcane constructions from any number of academic papers written in the past 10 years, and

> the argument—such as it is—evaporates. But the situation is not
> much better elsewhere in the academy, where thought is often
> fenced in by disciplinary jargon. (696)

Not only does Orr mischaracterize postmodernism and post-structuralism, but he doesn't explain, for instance, why the "contempt for clarity" is "pseudo-intellectual" rather than just intellectual, or how "careful argument" has been jettisoned by proponents of postmodernism and poststructuralism. I won't belabor the point that Orr's clear prose is hardly a model of careful argument, but I want to note the mechanism that makes postmodernism and deconstruction objects of the whipping post. Orr goes on to make his allegiances even clearer:

> we are no longer held together, as we once were, by the reading
> of a common literature or by listening to great stories, and so we
> cannot draw on a common set of metaphors and images as we
> once did. Allusions to the Bible and other great books no longer
> resonate because they are simply unfamiliar to a growing num-
> ber of people. (698–99)

He concludes his article with this admonition:

> We must instill in our students an appreciation for language, lit-
> erature, and words well crafted and used to good ends. As teach-
> ers we should insist on good writing. We should assign books and
> readings that are well written. We should restore rhetoric—the
> ability to speak clearly and well—to the liberal arts curriculum.
> Our own speaking and writing ought to demonstrate clarity and
> truthfulness. (28–29)

On the one side of Orr's neat binary, we have clarity, good writing, truth, the canon, and the Bible. On the other, deconstruction, postmodernism, young people, technology (email), and bad writing. Note how the lineup is ideological rather than logical: the Bible and canonical literature are not necessarily models of clarity—given their often highly metaphoric styles and the multiple conflicting interpretations they continue to engender—yet, alongside "truth," they come to stand for particular political, philosophical, and pedagogical epistemologies.

The above examples are representative of the texts and assumptions of many other contemporary scholarly and lay commentators, who represent their championing of clarity as matter-of-fact, even though this matter-of-factness is in itself constructed by contested philosophical and political allegiances. Not all calls for clarity are as blatantly reactionary as Orr's, but these linkages do occur, with predictable frequency, in attacks on theory, difficult writing, and supposed lack of clarity. Not only are complex prose, vocabulary, and ideas constructed as the antithesis of clarity, but theory itself becomes the object of attack. Additionally, composition theory has been subjected to this kind of conflation. Gary Olson points out the ways in which the rise of theoretical scholarship in our discipline was met with attacks, not only on the theoretical enterprise itself, but also on the language in which this scholarship was written (Olson 2002, 23). In an article entitled "Textbookspeak," William Lutz (1996) attacks the language of composition studies as needlessly inflated in order to make something simple seem more important; Lutz insists, "Teaching writing isn't all that complex . . . it's not brain surgery." Here we see, quite explicitly, how the critique of language is imbricated in a particular worldview and intellectual position, and in the renunciation of conflicting views/positions. Lutz's argument makes at least two questionable assumptions: a) composition theory is only concerned with the teaching of writing, and b) the teaching of writing is a simple undertaking. Both of these assumptions have been contested by theorists and teachers of composition, but Lutz addresses these substantive issues only obliquely, via a denunciation of the language in which these appeals are made.

Once again, with Lutz, hostility to theory—or to the particular dispositions advocated in this theory—masquerades as criticism of poor writing. I could cite many other examples of attacks on theory that are, in some way or another, explicitly or implicitly, similar to Orr's, Lutz's, or those cited by Olson.[5] On the face of it, these complaints are often directed only at the writing styles of theorists; in effect, they are ideological reactions against the theoretical enterprise itself and the values espoused in it. These may include Marxism (Jameson) and other radical political critiques of liberalism and humanism, as well as poststructuralist destabilizations of foundationalist epistemologies, unified subjects, master narratives, referential language, and singular meaning. Cathy Birkenstein points out how even some attacks on Butler's "award winning" bad writing take strong issue with Butler's arguments (Birkenstein 2010, 270), belying critics' claims that Butler's prose is incomprehensible, and hinting that it is actually Butler's philosophical and political positions that are the source of outrage. Lynn Worsham argues that "political" interpretation of *écriture féminine*, which denies the radical postmodernism of *écriture féminine*, "begins as a quest for meaning and ends as phallocentric obsession with one meaning" (Worsham 1991, 84). Clarity's comfort can be symptomatic of a parallel anxiety/desire to fix and control meaning in the face of challenges to such fixity and control.

In addition, I hope that the examples I have briefly discussed demonstrate that clarity is not as self-evident as its proponents like to think—in fact, the very proponents of clarity often use strikingly "clear" language to convey arguments that are convoluted, misleading, and enigmatic. In the above quote from Orr, for instance, the assumptions that "we were once held together" and that being "held together" is a good thing, as well as the failure to unpack who "we" is, are telling demonstrations of sleight-of-hand presented as and in the name of clarity. In their introduction to the anthology *Just Being Difficult: Academic Writing in the Public Arena*, Jonathan Culler and Kevin Lamb point out that the charge of "bad writing" against scholars in the humanities is usually made without any explanation of why or how their writing is "bad," as if merely quoting a portion of the offending prose is proof in and of itself: "The allegation of *bad writing* works . . . through an appeal to transparency that assigns badness to opacity. But if the most credible gloss for *bad* in *bad writing* is simply 'unclear,' doesn't the word itself—as an unclear substitution for the word *unclear*—enact the same failure of clarity it decries?" (Culler and Lamb 2003a, 2).[6] Judith Butler carries the contradictions of clarity a step further by examining a metonymic instance of clarity's content:

> The demand for lucidity forgets the ruses that motor the ostensi-
> bly "clear" view. Avital Ronell recalls the moment in which Nixon
> looked into the eyes of the nation and said, "let me make one thing
> perfectly clear" and then proceeded to lie. What travels under the
> sign of "clarity," and what would be the price of failing to deploy a
> certain critical suspicion when the arrival of lucidity is announced?
> Who devises the protocols of "clarity" and whose interests do they
> serve? What is foreclosed by the insistence on parochial standards
> of transparency as requisite for all communication? What does
> "transparency" keep obscure? (Butler 1999, xix)

Clarity, then, can be duplicity or obscurity, the very things it
purports to rectify, whether maliciously (as with Nixon) or
innocently.

As I suggested earlier, not all demands for and defenses of
clarity emanate from right-wing politics, and, certainly, not all
advocates of clarity are anti-theory ideologues. Gerald Graff, for
example, critiques "academese," obfuscation, and opacity, and
calls for clarity in academic writing in *Clueless in Academe* (Graff
2003). Not only does his book avoid bashing theory, but Graff
himself is well-known for his engagements with and explications
of critical theory. (Graff also argues that academic writing isn't
necessarily as difficult as it is made out to be.) However, it is
important to consider the *results* of diverse insistences on clarity, to trace the (unwitting) collusions among these insistences,
and to revisit the ways in which apparently opposite political
ideologies can make common cause around pedagogy and
the construction of students. Asao Inoue's "Community-Based
Assessment Pedagogy" is an instructive case in point: while
Inoue's discussion of the problems with traditional paradigms
of grading composition could signal a dissident disposition,
Inoue nevertheless repeatedly resorts to clarity as a desirable
assessment criterion (Inoue 2005, 217–219). He also uses his
appeal for clarity to explain his manipulation of student quotes
in the article (226), an instance, perhaps, of what Worsham—
describing literacy's alignment "with the ideology of the clear
and distinct"—might see as literacy's "power to recuperate the
power of those already in a position to order and give meaning to the social world" (Worsham 1991, 93). This is also a

suggestive exemplification of how clarity's disciplining function in the theory wars might be intricated with power relations in the composition classroom.

Birkenstein's (2010) defense of Judith Butler's prose in the former's *College English* article "We Got the Wrong Gal: Rethinking the 'Bad' Academic Writing of Judith Butler" demonstrates how the displacements I have been chronicling in this chapter might be used in the service of theory detraction, as much as they may be deployed in defense of theory. While I am happy to see Birkenstein defending Butler's writing, I am less sanguine about her attempt to rehabilitate Butler by making the case that Butler's prose is actually clear, after all. First, such an argument reproduces the clear/unclear binary, and implies that there *is* such a thing as "clarity," if we just look carefully enough. I have been arguing that the notion of clarity is an obfuscation, and so, from my perspective, it makes no sense to parse out what is clear and what isn't. "Clarity" always stands for something else. And second, Birkenstein's defense of Butler becomes as restrictive as the original attacks on Butler by creating a new binary that positions Butler on the "good" side of academic writing, and "much academic writing" that lacks a "clear, overarching argument or thesis" or "discernible argument or point" on the "bad" (Birkenstein 2010, 275, 281). I will have plenty more to say about thesis imperatives in chapter 6 (audience), but for now note how Birkenstein's need to place Butler on the side of clarity enables her to prescribe a reductive model of academic writing that—as Birkenstein herself admits—in fact contradicts Butler's and others' stated rationales for "difficult" prose that embodies challenges to conventional epistemologies and forms. Prescriptive models such as Birkenstein's often inform and are informed by theories and practices of composition pedagogy, and certainly Birkenstein's defense of Butler is in line with the model of academic writing offered in the popular textbook authored by Graff and Birkenstein (2010), *They Say, I Say: The Moves That Matter in Academic Writing*.

I turn to the collisions and intersections among theory, pedagogy, and disparate ideological affiliations in the following section. While there may not be a direct or obvious connection between attacks on theory and the call for clarity in student writing, I want to frame pedagogy and student writing within the context of critiques of obscurantism in published scholarly writing. I want to be evocative, to impel compositionists to think of clarity itself as a problem, to ponder the ways in which unreflective invocations of clarity in the classroom can complement theory-bashing (and even defenses of theory) and bring about similar results in their joint reliance on axiom and indefinition, albeit the impetuses for the two deployments of clarity may be quite different.

III. PEDAGOGICAL CONSEQUENCE

The ways in which demands for clarity often converge with covert resistance to poststructuralist epistemologies inform telling sets of contradictions in the composition classroom, where students are constructed and instructed in particular patterns informed by the ideologies allied with clarity. Here I elaborate several interlocking sites where clarity imperatives play out in the composition classroom, and what I see as the implications of these imperatives in the context of the anti-theory discourses discussed above—that these sites reveal disjunctions between composition theory and the teaching of writing around clarity's taken-for-grantedness, the status of student writers, and the purposes of composition courses.

Despite the professed zeal for clarity in student writing among many composition stakeholders (teachers, administrators, theorists, and even students), critical and composition theorists have defended difficult writing and critiqued attacks on difficult writing—and, as I've already indicated, it's hard to avoid veiwing clarity as the other of difficult writing. In addition to work by cultural critics and critical theorists (Culler and Lamb 2003b) that has treated the problem of difficulty in interesting and productive ways, scholars in rhetoric and composition—such as Sarah Arroyo (2003), Diane Davis (2000), Lester Faigley (1992), Gary Olson (1991, 2002, 2008), Victor

Vitanza (1991), and Lynn Worsham (1991, 2002)—have written in "difficult" language and/or have addressed, sympathetically, difficult writing, as have two recent issues of *jac*. In one of those issues, Christa Albrecht-Crane argues that, in a culture that emphasizes brevity, superficiality, and commodification, difficulty resists efficiency and utilitarianism (Albrecht-Crane 2003, 857). James Kastely's *jac* article, "The Earned Increment: Kenneth Burke's Argument for Inefficiency," sees difficulty in writing as a critique of efficiency and productivity and a resistance to appropriation (Kastely 2003).[7] While I do not wish to reduce all "difficult" (or all "clear") writing to a singular effect and meaning, I want to point to some possible implications of prose style that seem to escape monodirectional calls for clarity, as well as to a disjunction between, on the one hand, current scholarship in the field and, on the other, composition pedagogy and discourse about composition pedagogy. This is one of the many lags between contemporary critical theory and writing classroom practice, one of the gaps between the scholarship in our discipline and the teaching that we often think of as enacting that scholarship, since both the uncritical denigration of difficult writing in critical theory and the unreflective insistence on clarity in student writing evidence no engagement with the arguments advanced in this scholarship.

This gap manifests itself in a high culture/low culture binary that plays out in theories and practices of reading, as well as in differing attitudes to student writing compared to the work of published authors, despite imperatives in the field that students be interpellated into composition as "real writers" (see axiom 4 from chapter 1). There is often a contradiction between the writing we enjoy reading—and expect our students to acquire a taste for—and the writing we insist our students produce. The former might be full of ambiguous and complex content and convoluted, difficult, unconventional prose. While we are willing to recognize—and even enjoy—the work that goes into reading difficult fiction and nonfiction texts by professional writers, when it comes to our own students' writing, sometimes neither we nor our students have the time or willingness to engage in that kind of work. These texts must be clear and easy to read, two concepts that often become interchangeable. Alas, students quickly pick up on this from us and become eager to judge all writing—both peer and professional—based on how easy it is to read. They may use their experience of finding a text difficult to read as reason to dismiss or criticize the text, rather than seeing this difficulty as exposing their own deficiencies, or as presenting a productive intellectual challenge to them as readers and writers. Not understanding becomes a position of power from which to attack the text (Culler and Lamb 2003a, 3). We can't blame students for this anti-intellectualism if we continue to repeat the mantra of clarity when it comes to their own writing.

To further complicate matters, some writing teachers want their students to immerse themselves in the writing conventions of a particular discipline, area of inquiry, or profession, though their insistence on clarity inevitably includes injunctions against jargon, the very marks of topic-, discipline-, and profession-specific writing.[8] Rebecca Moore Howard (1999) makes the powerful argument that the academy's obsession with plagiarism signals its attempts at gate-keeping, at preventing students from entering into the academic and professional discourse communities they must become a part of in order to succeed. The same point could surely be made about strictures against jargon—and the demand for clarity—in student writing: they reinforce hierarchies that fix students' places as students rather than writers, as fake academics rather than professionals.

Demands for clarity in student writing might not only be informed by assumptions about readability and reader-friendliness, but also, more parochially, by the politics of instructors' time and patience. Min-Zhan Lu's (1994) daring suggestion that student texts deserve the same kind of close reading and generous interpretation of ambiguity accorded work by published writers[9] is frequently countered by resorting to the question of student intent (despite the fact that literary theory discredited authorial intent as a foundation for the interpretation of literature over four decades ago—more on this in the next chapter) or protestations about teacher workload. The disposition of efficiency in relation to student texts marks the confluence of the ideologies of efficiency and utilitarianism critiqued by Albrecht-Crane (2003) and Kastely (2003). With the material realities of a professional underclass (composition instructors) who are overworked and undervalued, and who often cannot afford the luxury of leisurely readings of student texts, these ideologies and materialities mutually reinforce one another. But efficiency mandates also speak to the larger value placed on the (sub)discipline of composition as a whole. Despite valiant efforts by compositionists over the last two decades to contest the diminution of composition as merely a service field, composition continues to be defined as a handmaiden to other disciplines and fields.[10] The recent efforts of past Modern Language Association (MLA) President Gerald Graff to bring "writing in from the cold" might be seen as merely consolidating that marginalization. Commenting on the injustices of the contingent faculty labor system in US academia, Graff advises,

> The word also needs to get out that the two-track system lowers the quality of education, not least because it widens the disconnections between writing courses and the literature and other subject matter courses taught by the regular faculty. At most universities there tends to be little communication between the composition program and the disciplinary faculty about what is wanted or expected in student writing. Faculty members in the disciplines rarely have a clear idea of the philosophy of writing informing the composition program, while composition teachers (through no fault of theirs) tend to be equally in the dark about what instructors in the disciplines look for in their writing assignments—assuming they give some. (Graff 2008, 3)

Note how, in Graff's formulation, not only is composition not a "subject matter" or "discipline," but it can only be imagined as serving to prepare students for writing assignments in other classes (contrarily, it would be unthinkable to imagine literature classes as serving only to enable students to succeed in their composition courses). We might look, then, at the trajectory from Graff's criticism of "academese" to his inability to think of composition in a way other than utilitarian, and ask how these liberal interventions into academic practice and discourse ultimately collude with the anti-intellectualism and conservatism of anti-theory projects.

Efficiency and utility also seem to merge with functional views of higher education, usually well-meaning in their concern for students' interests and preferences, but often remarginalizing those who are already viewed in opposition to intellectualism and abstraction. I have taught at institutions where faculty were enjoined to develop intellectually rigorous curricula, yet at the same time we were reminded that—because these institutions are working class universities—the primary function of their programs should be to train students for the workforce. We are led to believe that this is what students want and what we are beholden to provide. In an interview, Noam Chomsky (2005) was asked about the growing "emphasis on the utilitarian value of higher education, the idea that people, especially poor people and people of color, need jobs and don't have time for this idea of educating the whole person." Chomsky's succinct response: "That's a point of view that belongs in dictatorships, not in democracies. It assumes that if you're poor, you don't have any need—there's no justification—for you to be offered the opportunity to participate in high culture. . . . that is garbage" (100).

In a *Chronicle of Higher Education* article, Ben Yagoda (2004) articulates a well-worn objection to my efforts to disrupt the opposition between critical theory and student writing, as well as between the published work of established writers and the texts of apprentice writers: "We all would grant that the singularity of Charles Dickens's or Dave Barry's prose is a good thing. But would it be wise—or sane—to suggest such singularity as a goal for the average English-composition student? We are not all destined to be Hemingways, nor would most of us want to be" (6). My response, in addition to insisting on the importance and productiveness of recognizing students as real writers, is that, even for students, there is value in working with interesting language as a means of coming to language and coming to

ideas. Paul Heilker's discussion of "essaying" versus "expository"
writing gives a compelling rationale for language ambitions on
language grounds alone: "one reason I want students to write
essays is I simply, selfishly, want more interesting things to read
from them. Clarity and order are virtues, no doubt, but over-
done they produce prose that is flat, predictable, and boring"
(Heilker 2006, 197).

We also need to think about how the insistence on clarity
restricts ideas and thinking, and might make impossible for
students the kind of complex thinking that critical theorists
aspire to. In addition to the value of language complexity in its
own right, then, there is value in students working with difficult
ideas and practicing—even if inexpertly—the kinds of complex
writing that embodies these ideas. In his critique of Joseph M.
Williams' advocacy of the "plain style," Ian Pringle points to evidence suggesting that not only when "students are going through
a period of . . . cognitive growth, striving for a new range in their
ability to form abstractions, their writing sometimes comes to
be extremely clumsy, almost indeed 'terminally opaque,'"[11] but
also that "what typical judges of student writing value when they
make their judgments is a complex style with heavier cognitive
demands" (Pringle 1983, 95–96). Surely inexpert complexity is
preferable to expert simplicity[12] if it is indicative of intellectual
wrestling and scholarly ambition rather than the complacency
of comfort? Sometimes writing that "doesn't work" is still interesting and productive. Why pretend that we aren't sometimes
entranced by writing that is mysterious, enigmatic, or illogical—
by writing over which the writer/reader does not always have
complete control? We so often complain about student essays
that are reductive, simplistic, or trite. To what extent are our
demands for clarity responsible for these problems? If we accept
that form and content are interconnected, if we are persuaded
by research in composition that shows how students' difficulties
with language in their writing often reflect problems with concepts or arguments, then we must also admit that working with
difficult language and difficulty working with language are an
integral part of exploring sophisticated ideas. If, as Jon Spayde

conflictedly laments/celebrates, French theory transformed how intellectuals look at nearly everything—"mostly by making everything more complex," by giving us "richer models of how we're formed by cultural and social forces," and by generating jargon-choked fusions of diverse disciplinary and political traditions (Spayde 2004, 76–77)—then perhaps jargon-choked prose should be rewarded for its ambition, for its challenges to readers and writers, and for its imbrication in critical thinking. Clarity in and of itself does not achieve any of these things.

IV. WRITING OUT OF BOUNDS

Critical theorists and their apologists have repeatedly discussed the need to find innovative language to convey new, complex, and difficult ideas (e.g., Butler 1999, xviii; Vitanza 1991, 159; Wells 2003, 492). Existing and conventional language structures may be inadequate to embody ideas that often critique language itself and the power structures that enform conventional language. These defenses of difficult writing have frequently been developed in response to proponents of writing clarity, who inevitably point to exemplars from critical theory, or just indict theory in general, when citing professional writing that lacks clarity. We need to ask, then, what kinds of ideas (and what kinds of writing) are being resisted in the name of clarity. We need to ask what values and institutions are being privileged, and what systems underlie these values and institutions. We need to ask what clarity really means. And we need to ask what "unclarity" means and what it does.

Writing that is demonized for its supposed lack of clarity may be "unclear" out of necessity and/or accident. It might work to create new or unconventional understandings, and ways of making them, recognizing in the process that strange language and innovative ways of using language must embody these understandings.[13] In this case, clarity could simply stand for the conventional, the known, the old (though it doesn't necessarily do so). New epistemologies are categorized with the moniker "unclear" precisely because they are unfamiliar. The jargon of a specific discipline, topic, or epistemology might include specialized language that is necessary for the sake of precision, or for the purpose of enabling writers and readers to take certain understandings for granted in order to move a discussion beyond the basics. To outsiders, this jargon may appear as willful obtuseness or a failure to write clearly.

For student writers in multimodal, postmodern, globalized composing spaces, a failure of clarity can indicate a grappling with new ideas and discourses as much as it might signal situatedness in these composing spaces. In the interstices where necessity and accident merge and change places, where authorial intent is neither discernible nor interesting, and/or where critical theory meets student writing, sometimes composition that escapes clarity's bounds gestures toward revelation. And, in the process, "clear" and "unclear" may switch places.

NOTES

1. I thank Ryan Skinnell for pointing me to Bawarshi's argument here.
2. Carol Poster (1998) similarly reads the favor Aristotle found in the eyes of rhetoricians and compositionists in the twentieth century as a sign of the field's efforts to increase its prestige. For further discussion of the ways in which composition's work to legitimate itself as a field/discipline have circumscribed its compass, see Dobrin (2011) and Hawk (2007). Bizzell (2009, 494–95) also sees as part of this legitimizing effort cognitive work in composition by Linda Flower and colleagues, who developed "inner-directed" models of writing, and attempts to make composition research "scientific."
3. For a brief history of the discourse of plain style, as well as a defense of plain style, see Pounds (1987).
4. For more information about this "contest," see Culler and Lamb (2003a).
5. See Jennifer Howard (2005) for a discussion of the attacks against theory and "jargon" in the context of the supposed "devolution of theory" at the beginning of the twenty-first century. Howard also cites D.G. Myers' 1999 article "Bad Writing," reprinted in the 2005 anthology, *Theory's Empire: An Anthology of Dissent* (Patai and Corral 2005).
6. Albrecht-Crane (2003, 860) also cautions against "the dangerous conflation of clear prose with an assumed straightforward transmission of clear, simple ideas."
7. For further critique of instrumentalism and efficiency as university priorities, see Spellmeyer (1993).
8. Culler and Lamb (2003a, 2) argue that the demand for "clarity" is made specifically of scholarly writing in the humanities, and is indicative of

assumptions that scholarship in the humanities—unlike work in the sciences or social sciences—should be accessible to all. For a spirited defense of jargon, see Olson (2002).

9. Mariolina Salvatori and Patricia Donahue's innovative text book, *The Elements (and Pleasures) of Difficulty* (Salvatori and Donahue 2004), does admirable work in developing complex readings of student texts. However, while the book is careful to show students how to work with "difficult" literature and undertake "difficult" writing assignments—and the value of such work—it does not attend to "difficult" student texts. This aporia further supports the hierarchy that allows for and even celebrates difficult "literature," while assuming that student writing should be "straightforward."

10. For some critiques of this emphasis on composition's service function, see Colomb (2010), Dobrin (2011), Schilb (1996), and Zebroski (2011).

11. See Bartholomae (2001, especially 522) for further discussion of this argument.

12. Thanks to Aneil Rallin for reminding me of this point.

13. See Worsham (1991, 86) for a discussion of *écriture féminine* doing "subversive work" on language.

3

INTENT

For writing, like a game that defies its own rules, is an ongoing practice that may be said to be concerned, not with inserting a "me" into language, but with creating an opening where the "me" disappears while "I" endlessly come and go, as the nature of language requires. To confer an Author on a text is to close the writing.

(Trinh T. Minh-ha 1989, 35)

The issue of writerly intent and its role in readers' response to and interpretation of texts marks a fracture that is particularly telling of the dysfunctional ways in which student writers are often constructed in composition theory and pedagogy. In this chapter I investigate several dichotomies that structure this fracture (literature versus composition, theory versus pedagogy, fiction versus nonfiction, students versus authors), and suggest some theoretical and practical problems for composition because of its attachment to authorial intent, as well as some possibilities for a twenty-first century composition pedagogy.

I'll begin by invoking the specter of authorial intent in literary theory and pedagogy in order to establish both the limits of composition's own engagement with the question of intent (and with critical theory more generally) and the continuities between composition and literature, as evidenced in the disjunctions between theory and pedagogy in each. Section II attempts to account for the resilience of appeals to authorial intent in composition pedagogy (and some composition theory), despite the discrediting of such appeals by critical theory (and some composition theory). I conclude by asking what writing and pedagogical possibilities are foreclosed by these appeals, and how a depriviliging of intent as a commonplace

DOI: 10.7330/9780874219470.c003

might affect composition students, teachers, and writing (section III). Ultimately, I hope that by taking up Marilyn Cooper's invitation to consider the question, "How do writers and readers develop ideas together?" (Cooper 1986, 372), we can reimagine the ways in which texts of all kinds work in the composition classroom, and thus also rework the pedagogies that interpolate these texts inside (and outside) the classroom.

I. INTENT'S DEMISE

In literary studies, the commonplace that a text's meaning should be determined primarily in the context of the author's intent was famously debunked by Wimsatt and Beardsley's (1989) "Intentional Fallacy" as early as 1946, an assault on conventional assumptions about textual interpretation that was—despite the many shattering differences between New Criticism and poststructuralism—developed and complicated by structuralist and poststructuralist theory, including much-anthologized essays such as Barthes' 1967 article "The Death of the Author" (Barthes 1998) and Foucault's 1969 text "What is an Author?" (Foucault 1988).[1] These and other movements in critical and literary theory, including the rise of reader-response criticism in the 1970s, argued that readers, not authors, determine the meaning of texts; that authors don't (and shouldn't) have control over their meanings; that an understanding of subjectivity as fragmented, partial, and inconstant undercuts the conception of a unitary, univocal, rational, autonomous authorial self; that history and culture have a greater role in a text's meaning than an individual author's intent; that the social nature of language escapes the author's use and control of it; that language inscribes the author, rather than vice versa; that texts often belie their authors' intentions; that authors may not know what meanings their texts embody; that authors may achieve things they didn't intend; that they may not remember their intent; that they may (consciously or not) misrepresent their intention; and that, in any case, readers have no way of ascertaining an author's intent. This is not to say that the possibility of authorial intent should never be taken into consideration in the process of reading and interpreting texts. However, while knowledge of an author's putative intent may enrich a reader's engagement with and understanding of the author's text, all the skeptics of models of interpretation that privilege authorial intent agree that such a privileging is reductive and inaccurate. It impoverishes our readings of texts and the ways they function in culture and society, it doesn't fully allow for the power of language to construct realities, and it doesn't adequately account for how we make meaning and how texts circulate in culture.

Needless to say, these theoretical understandings have not been seamlessly translated into literature classrooms. The narrator of Laurie Halse Anderson's young adult novel *Speak* succinctly illustrates intent's entrenchment in many such classes in her parody of her high school English teacher's lesson on *The Scarlet Letter*: "It's all about SYMBOLISM, says Hairwoman. Every word chosen by Nathaniel, every comma, every paragraph break—these were all done on purpose. To get a decent grade in her class, we have to figure out what he was really trying to say" (Anderson 1999, 100). Some students and faculty, whether out of habit, resistance, or ignorance, still may have recourse to such narrow discourses and constructions of authorial intent in their quest to find/create textual meaning. Some continue to value authorial intent because of their conscious or unconscious allegiances to liberal humanist ideologies of individualism—the invincibility of individual agency, or the allure of writers' specialness. Sometimes teachers' theoretically unsound pedagogy is less a sign of willful resistance to the reign of theory and more a mark of the disjunction between theoretical understandings and pedagogical practices that I mentioned in chapter 1, of not knowing how to translate theoretical understandings into pedagogical practice, of falling back on old models of teaching, of teaching the way we were taught.

As the passage from *Speak* suggests, the chasm is even more apparent in many K–12 classrooms, where textbooks, bureaucracies, inadequate professional development, and outdated teacher preparation programs mean that classroom practices are often many decades behind scholarship in English. And, as I argue throughout this book, the chasms multiply and deepen in the case of composition. First, composition theory itself is fractured and has not unequivocally announced the death of the author. Second, the disjunction between theory and pedagogy is larger and more consequential in composition classrooms (at all levels) than it is in literature classrooms—this is hardly surprising, given that critical theory revolutionized literary studies several decades before it made an impact on composition scholarship and pedagogy. Third, as in the case of literature pedagogy, composition pedagogy still seems to be rooted in intent. Composition's allegiance to authorial intent takes many forms, as I outline in the following section. These forms include an implicit privileging of intent in composition theory that treats writing instruction, well-meaning assumptions about best practices in commonplace directions for responding to student writing, and the dispositions and practices of many composition instructors and student writers.

II. INTENT'S RESILIENCE IN COMPOSITION

The ascendance of social constructionist theories of writing in composition studies,[2] as well as the work of composition-ists and linguists like Linda Brodkey (1996), Marilyn Cooper (1986), Sharon Crowley (1987), Janet Giltrow (2009), Rebecca Moore Howard (1999), Jasper Neel (1988), and Kurt Spellmeyer (1993)—which critique modernist assumptions about authorial solitariness, originality, and unity in composition pedagogy—would seem to complement scholarship in literary and cultural theory that destabilizes the Author, subject, and presence. Further, we might imagine that collaborative writing, a practice much theorized in composition and often practiced in composition classrooms, would muddy the meaning of intent, and that electronic technologies' dislocation of the "traditional subjectivities of classroom writers" (Faigley 1992, 200) would contribute to the erosion of allegiances to writerly intent. However, I will chronicle in this section the many ways intent seems to hold sway in composition pedagogy, albeit sometimes conflict-edly. Part of the attachment to authorial intent in the compo-sition classroom is no doubt a function of what Faigley termed composition's refusal to surrender "its belief in the writer as an autonomous self" in his analysis of composition's relation-ship to postmodernism (15). This refusal also informs composi-tion's modernist conceptualization of authorial voice, a subject I address in chapter 4.

The residual pervasiveness of the intent-effect is evident, for instance, in Joseph Harris's (2006) book *Rewriting: How to Do Things With Texts*. While Harris cites Borges, Barthes, and other postmodern/poststructuralist writers, and emphasizes that he encourages students to read complex texts in non-reductive ways and respond to each others' work as they would to these published professional texts, he nevertheless focuses peer feed-back on drafts of student writing around the question, "What is the author trying to get done in this essay?" (133). Here respon-dents are invited to privilege their second guessing of authorial intent over the realities of language, effect, response, and read-ers' construction of meaning. As Spellmeyer succinctly puts it, "the first lesson a writer ever learns (and the last one the text-books ever teach) is the absolute impossibility of 'saying what you meant to say'" (Spellmeyer 1993, 73). I will discuss the ped-agogical implications of textbook and classroom privileging of student intent in section III. For now, I want to note that such gestures seem to be fairly endemic to composition pedagogy, and that the double consciousness that informs Harris' argu-ment (the reversion to the humanist subject in the composition classroom in spite of the engagement with poststructuralism) is also quite common, as I explain below.

The return to intent in the everyday lives of composition teachers and students is often predicated on practical concerns and well-meaning affiliations, although the cumulative force of these iterations can serve to mark composition pedagogy as theoretically naïve in terms of its conceptualization of autho-rial intent. When a colleague and I recently met with a student as part of a capstone interview, we paradigmatically suggested to one another beforehand that we begin the discussion of the student's writing by asking, "What were you trying to say?" The assumption seems to be that if we can get to intent, we can get to all the other issues and/or problems in a particular piece of student writing, and that we can do so by preserving the student's "voice" (more on voice in the next chapter).

My own localized survey of the dispositions and pedagogical practices of composition faculty at California State University, Northridge (CSUN)—where I taught for ten years—suggests that my colleague and I are not alone in this assumption. In 2009, I conducted an anonymous paper survey of composition instructors in my English Department to determine what role authorial intent plays in their writing instruction and the ways they structure their composition classes. I placed the four-question survey in the campus mailboxes of ninety-seven composition instructors, with a cover note indicating that the survey was anonymous and requesting that respondents complete the survey and return it to my mailbox. The survey asked the instructors to circle "very important," "somewhat important," "not important," or "unimportant" in response to each question, and also included a place for comments at the end (see appendix). I received forty-three responses. I summarize the results in the table below.

Of the forty-three composition faculty members who responded to my survey, thirty-nine indicated that they thought it "very important" (twenty-four) or "somewhat important" (fifteen) to establish a student's intent in a piece of writing in order to provide effective feedback. One respondent used the space for comments to give a concise synopsis of the multivalent influence of intent in much composition pedagogy: "In order to provide effective feedback, it is essential to understand the writer's intention as a student, instructor, or professional writer." Another respondent confirmed the link between work on audience and purpose in composition studies and authorial intent, checking "very important" in response to all questions about the relative need to consider intent in the composition classroom, and adding the comment, "I start with audience and purpose."

Table 3.1 Survey of English Department Composition Faculty at California State University, Northridge

	Very important	Somewhat important	Not important/ unimportant
When responding (orally or in writing) to student writing, how important is it to you to establish the student's intention with the piece of writing in order to provide effective feedback?	24	15	3
When students give each other feedback on their paper drafts, how important to giving effective feedback is it that they establish the writer's intention with the paper?	18	20	4
When you discuss professional nonfiction texts (e.g., newspaper articles, essays published in readers) with your students, how important is it to try to figure out the author's intention in writing the piece?	26	12	3
When you discuss sample student papers with your classes, how important is it to address what the student was trying to achieve in the sample paper under discussion?	24	14	2

Significantly, several of my respondents indicated that they were fully aware of the injunctions against privileging authorial intent in literary and cultural theory, and of the contradictions inherent in their composition pedagogy. One wrote, "Perhaps I'm harsh, but I try to teach my students that outside the classroom, their writing will be judged as effective or not solely based on product, not intent. It doesn't seem to help them ultimately to emphasize intent." Two respondents advocated adopting a mix of the two seemingly contradictory positions. One wrote, "'Intent' is an important focus in comp. classes as is the intentional fallacy—both should be discussed at length," while another insisted, "What an author/writer intends is important; however, I believe the actual effect of a piece of writing on the reader—the reader's response to a piece of writing—is equally important." Despite these demurrals, however, an overwhelming majority of the composition faculty respondents indicated that authorial intent was an important component of their composition pedagogy.

These composition faculty members represent a mix of tenured and tenure-track faculty, lecturers, and graduate teaching associates, and all hold graduate degrees in various areas of English studies—composition, literature, linguistics, and creative writing. In other words, the faculty members at this public, comprehensive US university are not unlike the composition faculty at many other similar institutions.[3] How, then, might we account for the resilience of authorial intent in composition? I have already gestured toward part of the explanation—composition's attachment to the modernist subject. But why does this attachment persist? My survey respondents point to some of the reasons for this resilience, which I attempt to synthesize and categorize below.

Audience, Purpose, and Genre

The faculty member above who begins "with audience and purpose" suggests one possible reason for the accumulation of significance around authorial intent in composition: the fairly recent increased attention to audience and purpose as an important component of genre awareness and assignment fulfillment, as well as assumptions about the functionality of expository writing. Indeed, articulation of writerly purpose has become de rigueur in today's informed composition classroom (Faigley 1992, 153ff.). In discussions of fiction or poetry in literature classes, teachers seldom ask their students to focus on the purpose of the text in question, or the author's purpose in writing the text—the texts are seen as having value in and of themselves, in addition to, or even in spite of, any purpose that occasioned their production. But discussion of purpose has become increasingly important in the analysis of expository writing. When it comes to students' own writing, most composition teachers are well-meaning in their efforts to encourage students to think of the purpose of a particular text they are composing:

such reflection is supposed to make the writing more meaningful, more "real" for the student. In the reading of texts, though, purpose often gets conflated with intent, and comes to signal not so much an effect of the text itself, but extra-textual information about the author. And the homage to the functional colludes with the concept of composition-as-service that, as I mentioned in chapter 2, many compositionists have been vigorously resisting for several decades.[4]

Much of the energy around questions of purpose and audience have recently been gathered under the rubric of genre theory, and, indeed, the contradictions within composition when it comes to authorial intent seem to be represented in "new genre theory," which lays down an encouraging theoretical framework for understanding "how readers and writers develop ideas together," but then appears to fall back on old assumptions about intent when pedagogical application is at stake. Charles Bazerman, for instance, argues that genre determines common meanings (Bazerman 1997, 21–22) by suggesting that meaning is outside the control of the individual writer's intent. Anis Bawarshi agrees that writers are, to some extent, written, and that genre "both organizes and generates" (Bawarshi 2003, 8). However, both Bazerman and Bawarshi seem reluctant to jettison the belief in individual agency that is the corollary of intent, the former in his utilitarian claim, "In understanding what is afoot in the genre, why the genre is what it is, we become aware of the multiple social and psychological factors our utterance needs to speak to in order to be most effective" (Bazerman 1997, 23), and the latter in his desire to teach his students to master particular genres (Bawarshi 2003, chapter 6). Bawarshi sums up his pedagogical imperative: "Teachers can and should teach students how to identify and analyze genred positions of articulation so that students can locate themselves and begin to participate within these positions more meaningfully, critically, and dexterously" (146). Genre, here, becomes just one more tool students can use in order to more effectively control the texts they produce and the meanings of those texts.

Amy Devitt's influential article synthesizing recent work in genre theory, "Generalizing About Genre: New Conceptions of an Old Concept"—notwithstanding its nods to poststructuralism—embodies the difficulty genre theory has in freeing itself from writerly intent as a central interpretive and instructive epistemology. Devitt begins by noting the influence of Derrida on the "most recent understandings of genre" and emphasizes its social contexts (Devitt 1993, 573). However, I would argue that because, as Devitt notes, "the new conception of genre shifts the focus from effects . . . to sources of those effects" (573) in writing, and because it concerns the recuperation of the individual against charges that genres are overly deterministic (579), the "new conception of genre" can end up merely returning our focus to the author's intent. In revision, genre awareness can come to represent a way for writers to more successfully realize their original intent (582).

It seems, then, that attention to audience, purpose, and genre has given, even if inadvertently, new impetus to the dominance of authorial intent in composition. On the one hand, insistences around genre, purpose, and audience serve to document and entrench intent's place in composition pedagogy; on the other, they also become the rationale for the continued attachment to intent.

Reading

Another possible explanation for the endurance of intent as a framework for structuring writing and response in the composition classroom might lie in the special emphasis now placed on the reading of expository texts in composition classes, as well as the renewed attention to reading processes and pedagogy in general in composition studies, as documented by David Jolliffe (2007) in a *CCC* essay reviewing recent scholarship on reading pedagogy.[5] In the case of published professional readings, some of the focus on intent can no doubt be explained by the predominance of nonfiction texts in college composition classrooms (e.g., essays in ubiquitous readers developed for first-year composition courses; newspaper articles used to prompt discussion, analysis, and writing; scholarly secondary sources used by students in research papers). Teachers and students may rationalize their conflicting treatments of fiction versus nonfiction texts by relying on the assumption that writers of imaginative literature have less control over the meanings of their texts than essayists, or that expository writing is more obviously an expression of a writer's intent than, say, a novel or a poem is. However, these intuitions are as fallacious as those that equate meaning with intent in fictional texts, given poststructuralism's suspicion of "facts" and "truth," since, as recent attention to memoir and other hybrid forms suggests, the dividing lines between fiction and nonfiction are hardly clear-cut. In any case, poststructuralist critiques of language's supposedly transparent referentiality may apply to language per se (see, for example, Brodkey 1996), irrespective of the genre enforming that language. Writing is writing, according to axiom 3 from the introduction to this book.

While readings have always played a significant role in college composition classrooms—even when instructors eschew textbooks, they often envisage student-produced texts as the major reading of the course—the recent attention to processes of reading and reading instruction in composition scholarship and textbooks marks an exponential shift from product to process that is doing for reading what process theory did for writing half a century ago. The preface to *Reading Rhetorically* synthesizes the rationale for composition's attention to reading by explaining that the book is "shaped by the belief that students need explicit instruction in analytical reading, not because they have problems with reading, but because college writing assignments demand sophisticated ways of reading" (Bean et al. 2007, xiv). The problem of intent has mushroomed with this new emphasis on reading in the composition classroom, especially with the recognition that students' writing difficulties are often the results of problems with reading, that reading needs to be scaffolded, that students need to be taught how to read. For now, beliefs about the importance of intent in student writing are transferred to structured and assisted readings of published expository writing, which are gaining more pedagogical attention. My survey respondent who wrote, "In order to provide effective feedback, it is essential to understand the writer's intention as a student, instructor, or professional writer," points to the ways in which composition has created equivalencies among what might be seen as different genuses of writers in other disciplines or institutional settings. On the one hand, we could say that this continuity of writers in composition studies is informed by the sound argument that texts by professional writers should be read the same way student texts are read— this is part of composition's process of resisting the canonization of any texts or writers and undermining hierarchies that discourage students from identifying as writers (axiom 4). On the other hand, it also rests on the less compelling axiom discussed above that makes nonfiction somehow fundamentally different from "literature," which imputes different rhetorical techniques to authors in the two modes, therefore suggesting that different interpretive strategies are called for when engaging with expository texts (axiom 3). Thus, we might argue that, while we may not foreground authorial intent in the study of literature, the fact that we do so in the composition classroom outlines the foundationally different types of tasks and texts we are working with. The move to distinguish these two arenas is no doubt also tied to the recuperation of classical rhetoric by composition scholars in the second half of the twentieth century, to composition's efforts to legitimate itself as a discipline, and to the injunction against using literary texts as the main source of reading in composition classrooms while the field established itself as a unique scholarly and pedagogical specialty.[6]

From my own position as a composition instructor at CSUN, I saw this attention to reading enacted in the Expository Reading and Writing Course (ERWC) that California State University introduced into high schools across the state, purportedly in order to better prepare California high school students to meet the demands of college-level writing.[7] The course was developed by college and high school faculty, and the two groups collaborated in leading the workshops designed to prepare secondary school teachers to teach the new course and the principles embedded in it. This college/K–12 alignment illustrates institutional crossovers in composition pedagogy, as well as the ways in which college composition's current turn to reading and obsessive focus on persuasive writing is being enforced in K–12 settings.

A popular textbook that epitomizes the renewed attention to reading, *Reading Rhetorically*, is used in these workshops, and informs much of the philosophy of reading instruction in the assignment templates that constitute the basis of the ERWC. The book nicely illustrates the schizophrenic position composition inhabits with regard to intent. It seems theoretically grounded in recognizing "reading as an interactive process of composing meaning" (Bean et al. 2007, xiv) rather than constructing the goal of reading as merely the reader's dutiful discovery of the author's (intended) meaning, and in conceptualizing "persuasive strategies in a text" (20) rather than searching for the writer's conscious effort to realize a certain intent. By looking at the *effects* of rather than the *intentions* behind particular textual features, readers can read closely without making assumptions or circumscribing interpretation according to authorial intent. However, the book simultaneously incorporates the notion of the writer's purpose from composition, reading purpose in the strong sense of "authors having designs on their readers" (10). And, in chapter 3, "Listening to a Text," the book advises readers, "When you listen attentively to a text, you are reading with the grain, trying to understand it in the way the author intended," a prelude to a more skeptical reading of texts (36).

These reading strategies revolve around a false binary centered on authorial intent: one is either trying to read a text according to the author's intent or one is looking at what the author might not have intended. What is absent here is a recognition that each of these readings is a projection of the reader, and that writing is not always transparently autobiographical (a lesson that students of literature seem to understand better than composition students). Trinh's (1989) accusation, "Charged with intentionality, writing is therefore disclosing (a secret), and reading is believing" (30), points to the reductiveness of this kind of intentional conflation, to the conflicts between authors and their texts—textual movements "from the intended into the unexpected" (Spellmeyer 1993, 73)—that *Reading Rhetorically* seems to want to suppress. While it might be useful to read texts multiple times, first sympathetically and then skeptically, structuring these reading strategies around authorial intent not only misleads students into believing that intent is ascertainable and quantifiable, but also sets up the sympathetic reading of a text as the one that converges with the author's intent, a strategy that may prove particularly problematic when these templates are applied to the reading of student texts as well (more on this later). Thus, much of the ERWC course falls back on authorial intent when it analyzes mainly nonfiction texts, unwittingly encouraging students to make arguments about intent as they analyze particular rhetorical strategies or word choices. Given the connections the course makes between reading and writing, these strategies are then supposed to inform students' own writing.

Students versus Authors

In the above discussion, I alluded to the imperative in composition to construct students as "real" authors, but Amy Robillard suggests that it is precisely composition's failure to fulfill this imperative that has left the discipline in the prestructuralist past.[8] Robillard argues that conventional scholarly citation practices, such as the identification of students by first name only or the omission of student texts from the list of works cited, reinforce the student/author distinction that the field is invested in maintaining, despite its protestations to the contrary. Why do such separations continue to enform composition's construction of authorship? In her articles "*Young Scholars* Affecting Composition: A Challenge to Disciplinary Citation Practices" (Robillard 2006b) and "Students and Authors in Composition Scholarship" (Robillard 2006a), Robillard offers an explanation by charting the unique place of student writing in composition studies, noting, "Students of other disciplines do not reflect the nature of the field itself" and insisting that composition studies could not exist without students (Robillard 2006a, 42). Composition, then, must have its identity invested in the category of students if it is to explain its raison d'être in terms of student writing and its attendant objects of analysis (e.g., student voice, student learning, student subjectivity, and student interventions into the academy and sociality). After all, if students circumscribe composition, then we need to preserve our understandings of students as material beings in our classrooms, not as Author effects. If, as Sharon Crowley puts it, "liberal composition pedagogy insists that student identities *are* the subject of composition" (Crowley 1998, 227), then the student as liberal humanist subject must be retained/recuperated in order for composition studies to maintain its liberal affiliations and agendas, as well as its (contested) student-centered identity.

We can connect the apparatuses of composition pedagogy and its assumptions about student writing to this desire for students, and its corollary, the need to distinguish students from authors (contrary to axiom 4). After a discussion of Barthes and the ways in which authors lose control over their own texts, Robillard pointedly continues, "To insist on students' retaining control over their texts is to deny them authorial status" (Robillard 2006a, 48). Paradoxically, it is precisely composition's insistence on student agency that marks its failure to construct students as authors. Student textual control is intricated in many layers of composition pedagogy, including those that address revision, error, and process models of composing. Composition pedagogy's focus on the thesis statement, for instance, can be seen as implicated in this desire for textual control (on the part of both writers and readers). A successful thesis statement is supposed to signal the writer's fully-realized intent applied retroactively to a complete text, proving that the student writer has managed every detail of the text by marshalling it in the service of their thesis statement. Often the thesis statement is presented at the beginning of the text, even though it cannot be accounted for until after the text's end, thereby completing the subterfuge of premeditated mastery.

In the last section of this chapter, I will discuss the further implications of students "losing control" over their texts. For now, I want to highlight composition's need to define students as one explanation for its dependence on the outdated notions of subjectivity and agency upon which appeals to authorial intent often rely. However, student agency also holds meanings beyond those articulated by Robillard, so its denial encompasses more than the circumscription of composition's subjects, as I explain below.

Agency

Some of the critiques of poststructuralism's evacuation of authorial agency in literary studies (most famously, Barbara Christian's (1987) article "The Race for Theory") saw this removal as especially troubling in a historical moment when previously marginalized subjects were finally coming to voice, when literary canons in English studies were being challenged for their exclusions of white women writers and writers of color, and when literary studies was undergoing radical paradigm shifts as a result of these challenges.[9] Doesn't the death of the author come only after centuries of white male Western authorial consolidation? Should we call for the death of all authors when some are only now getting their chance in the sun? Aren't poststructuralist insistences on subjectivity as fragmented and constructed a way of warding off the decentering of white Western men by the Other? These are just some of the questions the critics asked.

A related argument might be made with regard to student agency in composition classrooms. Isn't it especially important that students who are beginning to gain confidence as writers feel that they can control their writing and can plan on having something to say as authors? In the context of questions such as these, might a poststructuralist destabilization of authorial intent signal a retreat for the field of composition—a return to the privileging of product over process, a re-erasure of questions of purpose and audience that have lately informed compositions' commitment to "real" writing, and, most importantly, a failure to honor the agency of student writers? The apologia, "Perhaps I'm harsh," that prefaces the comment of my survey respondent, who wrote "Perhaps I'm harsh, but I try to teach my students that outside the classroom, their writing will be judged as effective or not solely based on product, not intent. It doesn't seem to help them ultimately to emphasize intent," signals this intrication of intent with honoring student agency and subjectivity. This commitment might be said to most dramatically distinguish composition pedagogy from the teaching of literature, given many compositionists' attention to student work as primary texts in the composition classroom, and given composition's stated commitment to recognizing students as writers. The advocacy of student agency is also imbricated in the process movement and the political contexts of its emergence in the United States in the 1960s, which interrogated hierarchical education pedagogies and institutions (Faigley 1992, chapter 2)—some composition teachers have a sentimental and/or ideological attachment to that history.

These dispositions about agency and subjectivity shape pedagogy and frame the possibilities of response to student writing. Brooke Horvath's (1994) synthesis of prevailing imperatives regarding teachers' responses to student writing still holds true in composition classrooms today: as a rule, teachers are urged not to "appropriate" student texts; the goal of responding to student writing should (usually) be to help students develop what is already there. In my introduction, I discussed Horvath's warning to teachers against co-opting student texts, a warning that makes intent's discursive power quite explicit: "If this happens, students may too readily conclude that success depends not upon fully realizing one's intentions, fully conveying one's meaning, fully expressing one's feelings or actualizing one's voice, but upon aping the teacher" (210). Horvath goes on to connect intent with the liberal pluralist belief in the sanctity of "individual opinion," establishing the trajectory of "voice" that I will discuss in chapter 4: "Perhaps most inappropriate of all are comments posing veiled attacks on the student, her opinions and interests, her worth as a writer" (211).

Other than a knee-jerk, reactionary, anti-theory position that dismisses the problematization of authorial intent out-of-hand, there are several possible avenues of responsible response to these concerns. One might assert that, given its particular focus on students and pedagogy, composition studies is a special case, and that work in critical theory is not appropriate or relevant to composition pedagogy, or that composition studies suggests a critique of theory's focus on literature in English departments at US universities. One of my survey respondents seemed to be making the argument for composition as a special case in her justification of the apparent contradiction between composition pedagogy and literary/critical theory: "Yes, we're up to our eyebrows in what C. Brooks might call 'intentional fallacy,' but the emphasis on argument in our freshman comp curriculum makes author's intent/purpose key." Another response to these concerns might adapt some of the defenses of theory (e.g., Bhabha 1988; hooks 1989; Trinh 1985, 96–97) to argue that it would be patronizing, dishonest, and hypocritical to perpetuate the lie of student writers' agency while deconstructing authorial intent in the work of published authors, that such a dichotomization reinforces the very distinction between student writers and "real" writers that compositionists are committed to contesting.

It seems to me that compositionists might complement these political and theoretical framings of the debate by specifically asking what harm there might be for students and their writing in privileging authorial intent, and, conversely, what value there might be for students, student writing, and the teaching of writing if we were to abandon our attention to intent in the composition classroom. I address these questions in the following section.

III. SURPRISE

Up to this point I have traced the resilience of authorial intent in composition and discussed possible explanations for this resilience, which informs composition's identity and its cherished ideals. However, we also need to analyze the effects of this resilience on student writing and composition pedagogy—this will be where we make our own contributions to the discourses of intent, authorship, and subjectivity that are distinct from those of literature scholars. I suggest that, paradoxically, the honoring of intent creates specific theoretical and pedagogical barriers to student writing and revision. This is not to simplistically assume the possibility or efficacy of an uncomplicated and complete abandonment of intent-focused writing and response. Rather, any alternate apparatus must account for intent's recursivity and the intersectional implications of its hold on composition.

If the privileging of intent can come to limit what can be done with a published professional text, we must also recognize that it can do so with student writing. Deconstruction and other epistemological challenges to the linear trajectory author–text–meaning have shown us that sometimes the most interesting work with texts needs to bracket intent, even though students sometimes have a hard time imagining a literary or other text in ways that are at odds with their perception of the author's intent. In the composition classroom, intent is a product of particular material conditions, in addition to the ideological baggage discussed in the previous section. For students and their teachers, it is often especially difficult to bracket intent when they are talking about a classmate's work, when the author is sitting in front of them. Material, subject, agent. Why should we want to resist these identificatory urges?

Part of the problem with privileging authorial intent in student writing is that intent often becomes the bottom line that controls dispositions, pedagogies, and epistemologies of writing. It restricts response. When students are asked to respond to or analyze a fellow student's paper, it's often in order for the writer to ascertain if she successfully conveyed her intended meaning. And intent, it seems, must always be honored. This attitude derives from liberal pluralist ideologies of individual agency, and serves as a testament to US academia's incorporation of the mantra that no one has the right to question someone else's beliefs—everyone is entitled to their own opinion—or, the composition classroom version of this axiom: it doesn't matter what you say, as long as you say it well/convincingly.[10] To fail to honor intent appears to be taboo in the writing classroom, to fundamentally dishonor the implicit or explicit contract of trust and respect between student and teacher, as well as among students. So, sometimes any gesture that can appear to complicate, disregard, sideline, question, threaten, or undermine authorial intent is seen as hostile, pedagogically unsound, and socially inept.

On the other hand, what kinds of blockages to writing and revision does such reverence for authorial intent create? It might be helpful to recall and rework David Bartholomae's (in)famous response to Peter Elbow in the former's *CCC* article, "Writing with Teachers" (Bartholomae 1995). In making the argument for the political and pedagogical efficacy of teaching "academic" rather than "personal" writing, Bartholomae gives the example of the student whose "personal" writing moves the author to tears but seems rather clichéd to the teacher, and who would feel insulted if a teacher or fellow students were to question the text's authenticity or originality. Somehow personal voice is always immune to critique, and student intent often suffers the same fate. Bartholomae's point is that the student's "personal voice" is socially constructed—we are not born with these voices and the ideas that constitute them—but the ideology of US individualism works precisely to conceal the enabling of the personal by the social and political. Students usually want to (and do) believe that their "personal voice" is original and uniquely theirs (more on this topic in the next chapter). For Bartholomae, academic writing focuses on precisely analyzing the power relations that structure such ideologies, and so reveal the apparatuses that mask the socially constructed nature of "personal" writing. However, the investment in the "personal" can be a way of foreclosing critique. The honoring of authorial intent in student writing can serve a similar silencing function that not only precludes certain kinds of critique of the work, but also stifles the author's own development as a writer.

The lure of the author function thus situates respondents to student writing in theoretically and ideologically frustrated positions. Given composition's ubiquitous belief in the importance of student writers' intentions—and the obeisance to those intentions—teachers or fellow students who find a student's presumptive intent morally or politically objectionable are often faced with two unenviable options in their response. They might feel obligated to honor that intent, and so find themselves squirming ethically as they give a student advice on how to "improve," how to make a morally objectionable argument more persuasive. Or, if the teacher and/or students are advocates of critical pedagogy or engagé writing, they might find themselves trying to persuade the writer to change her intent. That battle entails a host of problems around the issues of critical pedagogy and student resistance that have been well-documented.[11]

The fetishization of intent also hedges in composition and composition pedagogy more generally. The problem with the kinds of teacher response to student writing that Horvath characterizes as informed consensus (see section II above) is that they do not account for instances where the respondent believes that the writer might benefit from rethinking her intent, or cases where an assignment's originating impetus might not offer a productive route for completion. Composition teachers come across cases like these all the time, and often suggest to student writers that they rethink their topic or thesis, sometimes under the guise of helping the student more fully realize their original intent, and sometimes in defiance of the obeisance to intent.

But what if student writers were not taught that the goal of revision was to more fully realize their initial intent? What if intent was also up for revision? Such an expectation might allow for a greater range of writing processes and revisions. Writers might imagine themselves as facilitating a diversity of possible meanings rather than as attempting to fix meaning ever more narrowly as they revise. Less focus on writerly intent might also initiate different kinds of pedagogical practices and dispositions. Teachers could encourage student readers to play with the language of their peers as much as they do with the language of published professional writers. Then, perhaps, exchanges of ideas wouldn't primarily be read as "veiled attacks" on the writer's "opinions and interests" (Horvath 1994, 211). Peer workshops might take on different functions and tones if writers imagined revision as an opportunity to pursue their colleagues' "misreadings" of their texts rather than as a duty to correct those misreadings. The bracketing of intent could ultimately make discussions and negotiations around student writers' meanings and potential meanings less threatening, thus more fully realizing the purpose and potential of revision itself.

Min-Zhan Lu's (1994) article "Professing Multiculturalism: The Politics of Style in the Contact Zone" addresses some of these ideas and suggests one model that might help us think about what such a pedagogy might look like. Lu, working specifically with the texts of students who are English Language Learners (or, to use her term, "borderland" writers), encourages her students (and readers) to resist viewing "aberrant" usage in these texts in terms of error, but instead see the productive possibilities of meaning in these non-standard forms— after all, Lu argues, this is the way we read innovative language forms in the published work of professional writers. Lu writes that she is interested in "complicating but not denying the relationship between style and the writer's knowledge of and experience with the conventions of written English" (451), suggesting that the student writer may come to new, previously unavailable realizations about her prose and the possibilities of language through this process of analysis. However, as the above quote suggests, Lu's article does not advocate ignoring student authors' intentions altogether. In fact, in some ways Lu's strategy might appear to be designed to enable writers to more fully articulate and/or realize their original intentions (by seeing the different connotations of various language possibilities, the student writer discussed in Lu's article is able to revise her text to more precisely convey her meaning, whether this meaning was her original intent or is something new). By encouraging teachers and students to see beyond conventions and expectations, Lu brackets intent for the duration of the particular discussion, allowing for meanings to develop from the student paper beyond those initially envisaged by most fellow students, and probably beyond some of those imagined by the writer. This kind of reading of student work draws attention to language as a generative site of meaning, and shows how language and readers produce meaning alongside writers. Such readings move beyond the composition commonplace that writers discover ideas in the act of writing, a valuable understanding that nevertheless still privileges the coherent author as writer and reader of her work, as maker of meaning.

Writing teachers at all grade levels might encourage students to reflect on their own writings—as well as the writings of other students—in terms of the suggestiveness of language, looking for interesting or surprising meanings that arise alongside, in addition to, or even despite what they think the author's intention might be, and inviting authors to pursue those meanings if they are resonant and productive. Many writing instructors enact some version of this practice already, persuaded by Donald Murray's idea of "writing as discovery" (Murray 2011), and recognizing that "Writing does not so much contribute to thinking as provide an occasion for thinking—or, more precisely, a substrate upon which thinking can grow" (Bizzell 2009, 486). Instructors encourage students to discover ideas as they write, ideas generated by the writing itself rather than pre-planned in an outline, ideas that may, indeed, supplement or contradict an original thesis or plan. In fact, many writing instructors see the pursuit of such discoveries as the central task of revision. Why is it, then, that we fall back on intent when the writing is done (for now)? And what would it mean to also look at finished products as spaces of discovery? First, it might embody a recognition of the permanently messy but exciting relationship between language and thought (Crowley 2009, 344), between language and reality, between writing and thought, and between writers and their thoughts/language/writing. These relationships constantly produce new meanings, and are never finite. Second, it would finally give the lie to the liberal humanist delusion of the unqualified efficacy and unlimited potentiality of individual agency—the writer as reviser who is better able to control her meaning, her language, her text.

Although I am less interested than Lu in honoring intent, I am not insisting that intent and student agency should be ignored altogether. If this were the case, we'd all be doing automatic writing and nothing else. While writing and revision can be (and inevitably are) about intent for the writer, revision should be about more than realizing one's original intent, and readers should recognize the ways in which their own reading practices are as social and unexplainable as the texts they interpret. Marilyn Cooper' question, "How do writers and readers develop ideas together?" (Cooper 1986, 372) speaks not only to the generating of ideas, but also to the interpretation of texts, suggesting the kinds of collaborations involved in writing in postmodern spaces, where readers, writers, texts, and their material, historical, and social contexts collide and intersect to produce meanings that can't always be controlled, and that are often unexpected. "In the classroom I envision," Lu explains, citing Cornell West, "the notion of 'intention' is presented as the decision of a writer who understands not only the 'central role of human agency' but also that such agency is often 'enacted under circumstances not of one's own choosing'" (Lu 1994, 447). Here intent takes on a very different meaning from its modernist homonym, given that it now encompasses contexts beyond and against the author. The bracketing of traditional authorial intent in this case does not signal a return to the reactionary formalism championed by the New Criticism, since this bracketing engages with the very sociality of authorship that the New Criticism suppressed. However, I would recast the somber tone of the last phrase of Lu's point so that it allows for a greater range of interpretation: while we are inscribed in language and the social relations that words describe and create, language also surprises. Readers surprise, too. Writers should be open to the possibilities of these surprises.

My claim is not so much that writers can or should write without intentions—indeed, my own metacommentary in this book suggests my impetus for control of this text, and certainly that I had a certain intention in mind as I (re)wrote it. My point, rather, is that readers can, do, and should interpret texts without privileging authors' (imagined) intentions, and that these interpretations might productively encourage those authors to reimagine (their) intent. Intent itself is as much a textual construction as the text's meanings that are generated from that intent. After all, what you might be reading as my intention in this book is itself a construction of language and convention, and my metacommentary may, in fact, be a retrospectively created fiction of intent based on readers' reports and editors' suggestions, or a decision on my part to create a particular intent in my text.

When the writer revises after incorporating readers' surprises, does she hold a new intent that must surely be realized by the revised text? I would say no. Writers can go a step further, recognizing that revision is not only a realization of an original and new intent, but also a creation of new and unforeseen meanings. In this sense there is only process. There can never be an intentionalized product. Intent should never be a bottom line. Even when a "final" paper is turned in, readers/teachers/graders may read things in it that the writer did not intend. They can't be sure. They won't always know where intent and effect overlay and converge. And they shouldn't lament the writer's inability to predict all meanings or their own uncertainty.

It seems to me that such an openness would truly unlock the radical possibilities of genre theory's insight that "Writers invent within genres and are themselves invented by genres" (Bawarshi 2003, 7). Writers always write within constraints, and these constraints both allow for the writer to create meaning as well as create meanings beyond the writer's control. If a writer has any intent that remains meaningful in the long term, it can only be, as D. Diane Davis puts it, to "aim to amplify the irreparable *instability* and extreme *vulnerability* to which any writing necessarily testifies" (Davis 2000, 139). Bawarshi, Davis, and Robillard all champion some formulation of worldly writing, the latter two lamenting the ways in which composition's ties to the modernist subject suture it to ideologies of individualism that thrust it away from the communal. If we can suspend our allegiances to authorial intent, Cooper's (1986) question about how writers and readers develop ideas together would find a response in a community literacy, where writer, reader, genre, and other political and social identifications and impositions intersect and overlay to create uneven meaning, not necessarily in the sense of a willed and controlled collaboration, but in a continuing interplay over time and space.

Recognizing the probability that readers will continue to create new meanings—even after "final" revision—may have startling implications for writing and teaching, and for the grading and evaluation of student writing. It might mean that rubrics have to be reconsidered. It might mean that we must acknowledge we are grading our reading of a text as much as was are grading an author's writing of it. It might mean that we can't grade student writing any more. And it might mean that we have to rethink our relationship to and representation of our own writing.

NOTES

1. For other articulations of the critique of authorial authority and the privileging of authorial intent, and arguments for and against this critique, see Bakhtin (1981), Belsey (1980), Burke (2008), Faigley (1992, chapter 1), Knapp and Michaels (1985), Miller (1989), and Trinh (1989, 29). Burke argues that, while there is a continuity between New Criticism and poststructuralist insistences on the irrelevance of authorial intent, Derrida has been misread as jettisoning intent altogether (Burke 2008, 134ff.). According to Burke, Derrida's position was that "Intention is to be recognized, and respected, but on condition that we accept that its structures will not be fully and ideally homogenous with what is said or written, that it is not always and everywhere completely adequate to the communicative act. . . . if authorial intentions are to be deconstructed it must be accepted that they are cardinally relevant and recognisable" (135–36).

2. See Faigley (1992, especially chapter 1) and Gee (2009) for accounts of this ascendance.

3. I do not claim that my survey respondents are representative of all composition faculty in the United States, but I do believe that their perspectives

on authorial intent represent some themes that are quite common in our field.

4.   For some critiques of the ideology of efficiency in composition, as well as of the emphasis on the functionality of student writing, see Albrecht-Crane (2003), Kastely (2003b), and Spellmeyer (1993).

5.   See also Adler-Kassner (2005), Jolliffe and Harl (2008), and Roskelly and Jolliffe (2008).

6.   See Brady (2008) and Ianetta (2010) for overviews and histories of the conflict between literature and composition, debates about literature's place in the composition classroom, and recent attempts to recuperate literature for composition.

7.   For more information on the ERWC, see http://www.calstate.edu/eap /englishcourse.

8.   I am grateful to an anonymous *Composition Forum* reviewer for pointing me in the direction of Robillard's arguments here, and for suggesting that I tackle some of the issues raised in this section.

9.   See Jarratt (2009, especially 1394) and hooks (1990) for efforts to complicate this binary.

10. Ellen Rooney (1989) notes in *Seductive Reasoning: Pluralism as the Problematic of Contemporary Literary Theory* that liberal pluralism allows for any opinion as long as it is compatible with liberal pluralism! For further discussion of liberal pluralism in the context of academia, see my article "Civility and Liberal Pluralism" (Barnard 2005). For a trenchant critique of efforts to separate form from content in composition, see Brodkey (1996).

11. See Gorzelsky (2009) for an overview of composition scholarship on critical pedagogy and student resistance to it.

4
VOICE

When students find their voice and understand the power and magic of words, they are capable of expressing a myriad of emotions: frustration, anger, sadness, joy, wonder, curiosity. Through writing, students allow teachers to gain insight into their lives and innermost thoughts. Through writing, students can also share their strongest memories, deepest fears and hope for the future. And in classrooms where writing is shared, empathy, acceptance and appreciation for others take hold. The benefits go far beyond academics. When students find their voice, they can often discover more about themselves and the people around them.

(Sherry Posnick-Goodwin 2009c)

Decided that to find her own voice would be negotiating against her joy. That's what the culture seemed to be trying to tell her to do. . . . Decided that since what she wanted to do was just to write, not to find her own voice, could and would write by using anyone's voice, anyone's text, whatever materials she wanted to use. . . . Played in every playground she found; no one can do that in a class or hierarchical society.

(Kathy Acker 1990, 117, 118)

Yet I-the-writer do not express (a) reality more than (a) reality impresses itself on me. Expresses me.

(Trinh T. Minh-ha 1989, 18)

Art would perhaps be authentic only when it had totally rid itself of the idea of authenticity—of the concept of being-so-and-not-otherwise.

(Theodor Adorno 1973, 217)

I. ELUSIVE AUTHENTICITY

In a *Los Angeles Times* review of Los Angeles Opera's infamous postmodern staging of Wagner's *Ring* cycle in the summer of

DOI: 10.7330/9780874219470.c004

2010, Ann Powers defended designer Achim Freyer's much-maligned use of masks in the production, noting that "much of today's most important mainstream and indie pop resides in a similarly fantastic realm, far from conventional emotional expression. Artists as diverse as Gaga, Kanye West, Of Montreal and Animal Collective use masks both visual and vocal to challenge the idea that human expression is ever really 'natural'" (Powers 2010). Many attendees found this *Ring*'s masks alienating, missing the warmth and directness they associated with the identification of the singers' and characters' voices with their unobstructed facial expressions. But the final scene of *Götterdämmerung* emphasized the opera's artifice by revealing the stage machinery and exposing the underbelly of the set—in a flash of bathetic white light, sets were upended and protective camouflage was hoisted away from on-stage conductors and cue-givers, a violent reminder that the opera's characters and mise-en-scène were no more "natural" than the projection of operatic voices across a huge theater.

For poststructuralists and postmodernists, no voice is "natural" in the sense that literal and metaphorical voices are consequences of and mediated by imitation, socialization, artifice, learning, bricolage, fracture, and technology. The ways in which voices are heard, read, understood, and interpreted are also not transparent—different audiences infer different meanings. A unitary audience might find different meanings at different times, and audiences may not be aware of how they are constructing meaning. Additionally, processes of reception impact the production of voice if we believe that a voice's meaning is elaborated when received by a reading/hearing/interpreting subject. (While a voice's composer can form a self-audience, meaning becomes magnified and multiplied in the processes of reception by other audiences.)

An "authentic voice" is as elusive as a "natural voice," and discourses of authenticity are equally as problematic ethically and politically as imperatives of naturalization. Authenticity and naturalness are often imagined interchangeably, and discourses around the two concepts may serve equivalent functions of enforcement and exclusion, concealing the construction of their values and taken-for-grantedness at the same time they present themselves as activating the social justice agenda of (liberal) multiculturalism.[1] While "authenticity" needs can become the means by which diversity is achieved (e.g., we need to hear from the "authentic others"), demands for "authenticity" can also be used to police identity, demonize hybridity, or justify ethnic cleansing.[2] In postcolonial power relations, they can fix identity, fetishize Otherness, and, following Johannes Fabian's (1983) theorization of time and the Other, lock the Third World subject into premodernity. Here, demands for authenticity are more consequential than in the case of the *Ring* groupies who want their opera singers in burlap and winged helmets (despite the fact that historical Viking helmets were hornless), since they—wittingly or unwittingly—collude with political, scholarly, and pedagogical imperialisms.

II. COMPOSITION'S HISTORY OF VOICE

Since the inception of composition studies as a scholarly field, voice has held an important place in theorizations of student writing and teaching practices. A student's development of individual writerly voice was often seen as mutually constitutive of her personal, intellectual, and social development, and this interdependence justified composition's place in school and college curricula, and validated composition's argument that writing is a preeminent mode of thinking and learning. According to Darsie Bowden, the first chronicled use of the idea of voice in composition studies occurred at the 1966 Dartmouth Conference (Bowden 2003, 286).[3] Following Lester Faigley's discussion of composition's refusal to embrace poststructuralism and its investments in the stable self, Faigley chronicles expressivist composition pedagogy's advocacy of "authentic voice," as defined by the work of Donald Stewart. According to Faigley, Stewart's championing of individualism as an antidote to social conformity led Stewart to connect expressionistic rhetoric and "the artistic triumphs of high modernism" (Faigley 1992, 17).

Randall Freisinger explains some of the other understandings of writing and the self that came to be associated with Stewart's conceptualization of voice:

> Donald Stewart, in the preface to his 1972 text *The Authentic Voice: A Pre-Writing Approach to Student Writing*, makes clear a pedagogical intent which had already begun to dominate writing instruction. Stewart asserts his conviction that "the primary goal of any writing course is self-discovery for the student and that the most visible indication of that self-discovery is the appearance, in the student's writing, of an authentic voice." (Freisinger 1994, 248)

Sharon Crowley similarly argues that developing students' personal voices has been one of the staple rationales used to justify US college composition requirements (cited in Bawarshi 2003, 147), and John Schilb—citing Edward Corbett's discussion of the emergence of "the cult of self-expression"—notes that composition studies in the 1970s and 1980s "pushed student writers to convey above all their allegedly unique temperament and voice" (Schilb 1996, 61).

The idea of students (and other writers) "finding their voice" or "coming to voice" continually served as a raison d'être for composition and creative writing pedagogy, and shaped the resulting pedagogy and criteria for evaluating student writing. Donald Murray's (1984) textbook *Write to Learn* continued the tradition articulated by Stewart, mystifying voice as magical and defining it in essentialist terms: "Voice is what I am" (126). The text treats voice as if it were an independent entity, urging students to "Hear the Voice of the Draft" and "Hear the Unwritten Voice," as well as offering tips on "Tuning the Voice," etc. This representation of voice as a character to be heard or "tuned" obfuscates the ways in which voice is constructed and produced, and, most importantly, the ways in which voice can change. Instead, voice is just there—was always there—waiting to be discovered, let loose, and refined. As Carl Klaus pointedly puts it, referring to composition and creative writing pedagogy and practice, "The myth of 'finding one's voice' strongly implies that once having found it, one will never lose it, never change it" (Klaus 2010, 58).

By the time Murray's work was published, poststructuralist skepticism of the unified humanist subject was already facilitating the development of theories of voice as socially constructed, critically interrogating ideologies of a unified, natural, innate, or authentic voice (e.g., Brodkey and Henry 1992). Compositionists influenced by poststructuralist ideas would add their own expertise on writing processes and pedagogies to these accounts of subjectivity, suggesting that, given writing's multiple-mediated status, the metaphor of "voice" might only be meaningful and productive if the concept of voice is denaturalized, destabilized, and interrogated in its imbrications with power relations.[4] How, and by whom, are some voices constituted as authentic, while others are not? How are voices acquired? Why do student writers use particular voices in the first place? What does authenticity mean and what does its valorization signify? What are the stakes in learning and unlearning particular voices, and in validating or criticizing particular voices? What does "voice" even mean? Isn't the term itself a product of the very ideologies whose values it often enshrines? An essentialist conception of voice is dependent on a humanist understanding of the subject, since voice is presumed to flow monolithically and "naturally" from this coherent subject. If the subject is neither unitary nor stable, then it cannot have a faithful and consistent voice that speaks to/from its essential self—especially in the exercise of a taught and technology-based practice like writing. Voice is even more elusive in electronic writing modes, given the collaborative nature of much digital media, dissolving boundaries between authors and readers, and endless revision possibilities defining always unstable texts (Bowden 2003, 295).

However, in keeping with the pattern I have described in the previous two chapters, these new understandings of subjectivity often made their way unevenly into composition, as evidenced both in composition textbooks and scholarship. As David Bartholomae put it, "Commonplaces are the 'controlling ideas' of our composition textbooks, textbooks that not only insist upon a set form for expository writing but a set view of public life" (Bartholomae 2001, 514). Composition scholars have used textbooks to trace the dominant embodiments of trends in composition fantasies, imperatives, and teaching. Often composed by leading composition scholars, yet under the auspices of publishers eager to appeal to entrenched beliefs, textbooks' habitation of the juncture between institutional imperatives and current research—together with their lag behind scholarship in the field—inevitably means they don't necessarily reflect the dispositions and pedagogies of composition scholars and teachers, though their hegemony in the classroom results in them inescapably informing teaching practices to some extent. Faigley captures textbooks' slippery power: "But if textbooks are not reliable sources of data for how writing is actually taught, they do reflect teachers' and program directors' decisions about how writing should be represented to students" (Faigley 1992, 133). In this chapter, in chapter 2, and in the ones that follow, I adopt one of the traditions of composition scholarship by using textbooks as a form of inventory: I treat composition textbooks as one form of documentation of composition commonplaces, of how theory and scholarship unevenly find their way into pedagogy, or—recognizing that textbooks are not always an accurate reflection of classroom practice—at least of the disjunctions between theory/scholarship and one form of official public representation of composition (i.e., textbooks).

One example of a 1980s textbook embodying competing and contradictory theories of voice is Wayne Booth and Marshall Gregory's *The Harper and Row Rhetoric* (Booth and Gregory 1987). The text symptomatically points to the destabilization of composition commonplaces about voice, while rehearsing the traces of those commonplaces. On the one hand, Booth and Gregory (a) recognize that one doesn't just have one voice, (b) assign students to write texts in many different voices, and (c) argue that one can learn voice. Yet, on the other hand, they urge students against writing something they don't believe, and insist that voice is "rooted in who we are" (260). These contrapuntal views on voice articulate a common belief that, although writers may use various avatars, all these avatars in some way express the writer's "true" self. Not only does Booth and Gregory's latter assertion assume that "who we are" is something singular, fixed, transparent, and identifiable, but it also implies a one-to-one correspondence between the voice(s) of a writer and their who-we-areness. Textbooks such as Booth and Gregory's also no doubt reflect the hopes of many writing teachers, whose romantic fantasies of student voice are imbricated in some of the other qualities they value in student writing (and writing in general, perhaps) and the teaching of composition. In his analysis of the 1985 collection *What Makes Writing Good*, Faigley notes "the strong preference for autobiographical essays" on the parts of the writing teachers who contributed their picks for excellent student writing to the anthology, as well as these teachers' characterizations of the exemplary writing as possessing honesty, integrity, and authenticity (Faigley 1992, 120–21).

Assaults on this confident sense of voice-as-identity made their mark in the National Council of Teachers of English's (NCTE) 1994 anthology of scholarship on the topic of voice, *Voices on Voice* (Yancey 1994b). As Kathleen Blake Yancey noted in her introduction to the volume, there was "considerable contention" around the issue of how voice is developed and re-created. Yancey then went on to list some of the conflicting conceptions of voice, including voice "as a reference for truth, for self" and voice "as myth" (Yancey 1994a, xviii). The collection showcased some of these conflicting views on voice, while also attempting to develop a rapprochement among the competing theories by suggesting the significance of common elements in them, or that the disagreements revolve around misunderstandings, misinterpretations, or semantic quibbles rather than around fundamental philosophical conflicts (Elbow 1994b; Yancey 1994a). Peter Elbow, a contributor to Yancey's volume and a prolific scholar on the topic of voice, made a similar gesture in the introduction to his own anthology, *Landmark Essays on Voice and Writing*, urging that instead of favoring one position over the other, we "make use of both approaches or lenses" in the voice-as-constructed/voice-as-authentic debate, while admitting he believes that the supposedly "naïve credulity about the power of sincere presence in texts . . . can be seen as not so naïve" (Elbow 1994a, xv, xix). These gestures may be signs of defensive attempts to co-opt radical challenges to traditional assumptions about "voice" by scholars and teachers wedded to a humanist understanding of subjectivity; they also suggest how effective these liberal pluralist gestures will be in ensuring the resilience of traditional ideologies of voice in the years ahead.

III. CONTEMPORARY CONTRADICTIONS

Where are we now in terms of voice, twenty years after the publication of *Voices on Voice*? On the one hand, essentialist conceptions of voice are still ubiquitous in composition scholarship and teaching. Some significant recent scholarship in composition studies continues to replay the contradictions enacted by Booth and Gregory: it clings to humanist conceptions of voice, despite feeling obligated to acknowledge the challenges to these conceptions of voice from poststructuralists and others. For instance, Lizbeth Bryant's (2005) book is promisingly titled *Voice as Process*, and Bryant acknowledges poststructuralist critiques of the humanist subject, recognizes that subjects own multiple voices, and declares that voices are constructed by writers (6). However, Bryant still appears to assume that we all have an authentic voice that is uniquely and truly our own—other voices are extensions of or additions to that essential primary voice. In her assertion, "Wrangling over students' right to their own voices or the primacy of academic discourse is the most germane to my teaching," Bryant reinscribes foundationalist ideologies of subjectivity, especially in the phrase "students' rights to their own voices" (4).[5] And by opposing this right to voice with "academic discourse," Bryant constructs academic discourse as alien and artificial against the student's more natural, original voice. The case studies in the book consistently fall back on this conceptualization of "native voice," and the back cover blurb for Bryant's book makes the assumptions in this dichotomy even more explicit by casting the conflict as a matter of "the native or the academic." The term "native" complements Bryant's own deployment of colonialism as a metaphor in order to conceptualize academia's appropriation of students' "native" voices (7), and reproduces problematic assumptions of nativism, originality, authenticity, and purity that have been vigorously contested by poststructuralist, postcolonial, feminist, critical race, and queer theory. The gesture to honor the native informant often accompanies the paternalistic glorification of the "noble savage," as well as the ghettoization of the informant to a space of pure alterity. As Trinh (1997) pointedly states,

> What can be more authentically other than an otherness by the other, herself? Yet every piece of cake given by the master comes with a double-edged blade. The Afrikaners are prompt in saying, "You can take a black man from the bush, but you can't take the bush from the black man." The place of the native is always well-delimited. . . . Otherness has its laws and interdictions. Since you can't take the bush from the black man, it is the bush that is consistently given back to him, and as things often turn out it is also this very bush that the black man shall make his exclusive territory. (417)[6]

Tom Romano's (2004) book, *Crafting Authentic Voice*, enacts a nostalgia for ontology that is similar to Bryant's. Like Bryant, Romano recognizes "the unease in some of academia about the term *voice*," acknowledges that voices are shaped by social and other factors, and admits that we all use/inhabit multiple voices. And, also like Bryant, Romano ultimately ignores these claims. However, Romano does so in favor of an even more overtly essentialist take on voice than Bryant, comparing it to "the writer's DNA," and insisting that the multiple voices he acknowledges "are part of our identity." Romano's allusion to writers "losing" their voices and their voices being "quelled" solidifies this association of voice with the writer's identity, and even the writer's embodiment. This understanding of voice is enacted in Romano's pedagogy: "Maybe the brightest moment for me as a writing teacher occurs when I see students quicken to the power of their voices" (Romano 2004, 5-7, 91). Here, the romantic view of the author is in full force. The verb "quicken" invokes the role of inspiration, genius, and solitary writing practices associated with the ideology of Authorship that, as I have discussed in previous chapters, poststructuralist and some composition theorists have vigorously sought to demystify. Additionally, the voices whose power propels student writing seem to be there waiting to be discovered, as opposed to voices that are learned, shaped, fractured, and changed.

In other cases, scholars don't even make the cursory nods to poststructuralism's challenges to conventional theories of voice. For example, in Diann Baecker's (2007) *Composition Forum* article about validating emotion in student writing, both Baecker and her students uncritically recapitulate modernist understandings of voice in their familiar rehearsals of the ways in which academic writing protocols supposedly stifle students' voices. In her meditation on the role of anger—and emotion more generally—in the writing classroom, Baecker notes by way of illustration how a collage assignment she uses with her students elicits "images of violence and anger to express the process of writing for a teacher." One student rails that his "inner voice" does not find its way into his classroom essays. What seems symptomatic about this narrative is the very fact that voice here is taken as given, a commonplace not in need of explication, and so can be used in the service of another argument. Neither Baecker nor her students seem to feel the need to unpack voice, to question the distinction between "inner" and "outer" voices, the "authenticity" or "naturalness" of the inner voice, nor the processes of its construction. Its existence is taken as a given, as is its unproblematic and unitrajectoral correspondence with the composing subject. Graff and Birkenstein reproduce this uninterrogated binary in their textbook, *They Say/I Say: The Moves That Matter in Academic Writing*, when they make a well-meaning promise to students: "we want to show you how you can write effective academic arguments while holding on to some of your own voice" (Graff and Birkenstein 2010, 121).

As the above instances illustrate, humanist understandings of voice are still very much with us, though often with demurrals and contradictions that betray the cracks in their once-confident belief in their own common sense. On the other hand, the uncritical prioritization and celebration of voice is now absent in some composition arenas. A striking feature of many contemporary composition textbooks, for instance, is that they don't mention voice at all (e.g., Anker 2007; Bullock et al. 2010; Kennedy et al. 2007; Nadell et al. 2003; Skwire and Skwire 2005).[7] This absence could signal a response to poststructuralist critiques of traditional representations of voice, a simple retreat from using a now-contested term, a kow-towing to recent imperatives to emphasize academic writing in composition classrooms (and the erroneous assumption that voice is irrelevant to such writing), or other factors.

In the previous chapter, I discussed current imperatives emphasizing academic writing in college and high school composition in the United States.[8] For some scholars, teachers, and students, the increased emphasis on academic writing and the concomitant denigration of personal writing in college composition classes in the past two decades has brought about a loss of "personal voice" in student writing, and it's understandable why, in the face of what they see as a new onslaught of formulaic and soulless academic writing,[9] some might wax nostalgic for old conceptions of voice, or might seek to find ways of reclaiming some form of these ideas (e.g., Romano 2004 and Bryant 2005 discussed above, Yancey 1994a in her introduction to *Voices on Voice*, and Elbow 1994b in the same volume). The contemporary textbooks that omit any discussion of voice form stark contrasts with the older textbooks by distinguished scholars that I discussed at the beginning of this chapter, which address voice (in hindsight, however problematically) at considerable length. Booth and Gregory's (1987) *Harper and Row Rhetoric*, for instance, devotes an entire chapter to voice, and Donald Murray's (1984) *Write to Learn* includes a section on voice as an integral component of the writing process in each of the book's six chapters. The shifting terrain of voice in textbooks is illustrated in Kennedy et al.'s (2007) *Writing and Revising: A Portable Guide*, which uses a structure and headings very similar to Murray's, but without the sections on voice. Both texts include chapters on the writing process, planning, drafting, and revising, though Murray's section urging students to "Hear the Voice of the Draft" is replaced in the later book with a section on "Targeting Academic Readers"—a sign not only of the recent increased attention to audience in composition, but also of the current hegemony of "academic writing" in the first-year composition classroom. When academic writing is counterposed to personal writing or narrative writing, the former is often constructed as more objective, neutral, balanced, and research-based, and less emotional (more on this in chapters 5–7). All of these terms have been, to some degree, implicated in discussions about voice, and so the academic/non-academic dualism situates voice on the side of the non-academic, despite the interrogation of the reason/emotion binary by feminism and postcolonialism; despite the impossibility of objectivity argued by poststructuralists, feminists, postcolonialists, and others; and as if carefully constructed voices don't inhabit all forms of academic writing.

IV. TOWARD A POSTSTRUCTURALIST UNDERSTANDING OF VOICE

When it comes to voice, are the only options the Scylla and Charybdis of theoretical naiveté or soulless prose? How might we resist discredited humanist understandings of voice without simply abandoning the concept of voice altogether? Besides the intellectual satisfaction of reconciling critical theory with pedagogical praxis, what are the possible benefits of enacting a poststructuralist understanding of voice in the composition classroom, especially given, on the one hand, the lack of theoretical sophistication and generic character of textbooks that don't treat voice at all, and, on the other, the ongoing resilience of traditional conceptualizations of voice in composition theory and pedagogy?

Some of the benefits of a reimagined concept of voice parallel the possibilities from jettisoning the privileging of authorial intent that I discussed in chapter 3. For instance, a less essentialist conception of voice might lead to less student resistance to revision. Students often become invested in writing as their "real" selves—usually at the urging of their composition teachers—and so come to see critiques of their work by teachers or peers as an attack on those real selves. This defensive position, as we know, is often not conducive to effective or pleasurable habits of revision, and, in fact, can create dispositions that are fundamentally hostile to revision as a principle and practice. Just as instructors and students have come to regard student intent as sacrosanct, so student "voice" can be fetishized in ways that reify texts and writing processes—if a student hasn't "found" her voice or if she has "lost" her voice in her writing, then the recovery/discovery of this voice is fantasized as the bottom-line of textual integrity by many a writing instructor; and if a teacher's or colleague's revision suggestions are seen as threatening a student's voice, then voice becomes the defense against revision, the guarantor of authenticity and student ownership of that text.

Academic writing as a genre might also benefit from a reconceptualization of voice. Student contempt for academic writing styles, conventions, and forms often stems from the view that academic writing is "inauthentic" or doesn't allow the student writer to express her "true self." Even theoretically-sophisticated textbooks reenact these kinds of problematic binaries. For instance, *The Allyn and Bacon Guide to Writing* is careful to denaturalize rigid prescriptions for academic essay writing (what the text calls "closed-form prose"), but nevertheless concludes its section on composing and revising with suggestions for using "open-form elements to create 'voice' in closed-form prose" (Ramage et al. 2003, 564). The quotation marks around the term "voice" here gesture toward the recognition of voice as a construct, but the thrust of the lesson still implies that traditional closed-form prose is somehow voiceless, as if academic voices weren't as mediated and "artificial" as any other voices. As I noted in chapter 3, this rather simplistic view of academic writing was famously and brilliantly deconstructed by David Bartholomae (1995) over fifteen years ago in "Writing with Teachers." And, as I suggested in the previous section of the current chapter, if questions of authenticity and subjectivity were interrogated or developed in critical and multiple ways in relation to writing, especially student writing, perhaps such binary distinctions between the academic and the non-academic, between real and fake, and between the self and the other would be less robust. Under such a regime, students might more comfortably insert themselves into the "academic" as they envisage all voices—including their "non-academic" voices—in development, in flux, and always contingent. The "home voice," "inner voice," or "authentic voice" should not be constructed as fixed or given. It, too, should be cultivated and seen as subject to growth, change, embellishment, and even abandonment. When all voices, not just academic ones, are in flux, then academic voices might seem less alien.

Disrupting static and unitary notions of voice and the self might also help to dissuade student writers and readers from the assumption that writing should sound like speaking and that an effective written text is one where the reader can hear that writer's voice, "just as if she were speaking." Despite the fact that careful transcriptions of speech have demonstrated that writing is quite different from speaking (e.g., Abercrombie 1963; Chafe and Tannen 1987; Purcell-Gates 2001; Tannen 1982), inexperienced student writers often rehearse the commonplace that writing should approximate speaking, and see it as a mark of praise to tell a writer that her text "sounds like" her speaking voice, or that they can "hear" her speaking when they read it. Because the word "voice" is so powerfully connected to speaking, it is still common for many voice theorists to link voice in writing to oral vocal performance. Even Brittenham and Hoeller, in their unusually thoughtful composition textbook *Key Words for Academic Writers*—and in an otherwise admirable poststructuralist unfolding of the meaning of voice in academic writing—still assume that voice is "the sight of sound" (Brittenham and Hoeller 2004, 187). But why would we want writing to mimic speaking in the first place? While some might believe the originary voice in speech is more valuable than all others, to relegate writing to the merely redundant would be to deny its recursivity and its role as originator of meaning that composition has staked so much on.

Concomitantly, a separation between speech and writing could help to undercut the mythology that writing, especially student writing, should be "clear," transparent, and instantly accessible—commonplaces I critiqued in chapter 2. While such demands cannot be made unproblematically of either speaking or writing, these demands are often seen as redundant in the case of speaking (which, even more than writing, is assumed to conjure someone's "real" voice), and are therefore applied a fortiori to writing when it is projected as a quasi-transcription of speech. These kinds of instrumentalist and reductive circumscriptions of writing collude with the anti-intellectualism that pervades much US political culture, and ultimately also reduces the kinds and number of benefits and pleasures that writing might bring to authors and readers. It is often the spaces where an author's/narrator's voices are compromised or enigmatic that attracts critics and readers to literary texts, and that make literature evocative and interesting. Extending axiom 4 from chapter 1 (Students Are Writers), why should composition students be denied similar satisfactions in language's uncertainties and writing's unpredictability in the name of transmitting a putatively stable, coherent, and fixed "inner" voice?

V. OBJECTIONS

One potential problem with acceding to poststructuralist understandings of subjectivity as non-foundational, non-unitary, and radically relative might be an appropriation of writerly voice by anything-goes pluralist politics. All voices are posited as equivalent, with no consideration of the material power relations that empower some voices and silence others, nor of the relative ethical imperatives of some voices over others.[10] Consequently, the voices that students cherish or, for some students, may be inhabited at considerable political cost, are relegated to an apolitical smorgasbord of voices from which any student may choose at any particular time. Composition pedagogy, then, would see

itself as teaching students how to create and use a variety of different voices and argue a variety of different positions, with little
concern for the ethical implications of those voices and positions, or for students' own material, historical, and other stakes
in particular voices.[11] If students aren't exhorted to find and
develop their "true" voices, are they merely to, cynically perhaps,
attempt to adopt whatever voice might appease their readers or
teachers, even if such voices were "dishonest" or misrepresented
their own beliefs? While a writer's voice is usually interpreted to
include tone, prose style, ethos, and the character of the narrative or writerly self, this question suggests that voice is not
easily separable from content: the subject of voice's utterances
often come to be as much associated with voice as the manner
of those utterances.[12] Particularly when voice is equated with
the essentialist self, demands for honesty and authenticity can
apply to the signification of the writer's words no less than to the
character of the writer's voice, precisely as these two inseparable
components of discourse construct one another.

Following poststructuralism's debunking of "truth," charges
of moral relativism (misinformed, in my view) have defined left-
ist critiques of poststructuralism for several decades now, and
ludic understandings of voice in the composition classroom
might bolster such critiques. Concurrently, certain strains in
composition have seen their own versions of liberal pluralism
gain wide currency in (a) reactions against critical pedagogy;
(b) admonitions to composition faculty to desist from their
attention to issues around social justice and focus on form, not
content; (c) platitudes around the imperative to engage one's
opponents (or worse, to tell your reader whatever they want to
hear); and (d) taken-for-granted assumptions (reproduced by
students and teachers) that students should be free to argue any
position they choose, provided they argue it well (as if form and
content can be separated from one another so neatly). These
kinds of pedagogical practices promote disingenuity and moral
relativism, and fix composition only as the teaching of skills,
a relegation that many compositionists have been at pains to
contest for some time now. It would be ironic if compositionists

and others promoting these positions—who are often otherwise hostile to poststructuralist theory—were to harness poststructuralist understandings of voice in the service of such reactionary agendas.[13]

Other objections might be made to a poststructuralist understanding of voice along the lines of the critiques of the Author's dethronement that I articulated in the previous chapter, and that hinge on the question of student agency in composition classrooms. Compositionists have fought hard to legitimize student writing and student writers, and part of this process has involved authorizing students and student texts, promoting the concept of student ownership of writing as a significant component of students' construction of themselves as authors ("real" writers), and assigning that authorial presence the same degree of authenticity, authority, and legitimacy afforded professional writers (axiom 4). Composition teachers working with students of color, first generation college students, and other students who may not think of themselves as writers often see this ownership as an essential step toward these students' integration into and successful navigation of academic culture, as well as the sociality for which their academic careers are supposedly preparing them.[14] Encouraging a student to express her "authentic voice," to see her writing as a means to gain social subjectivity and even political agency for that voice, may become inextricably intricated with well-meaning impulses around ownership, authority, and resistance. In 2005 for instance, Cindy Moore articulated such a concern about giving up liberatory political assumptions around voice in a formulation strikingly similar to the attempt of the *Voices on Voice* anthology to reconcile traditional understandings of voice with postmodern critiques of it ten years earlier: "I think we can hold on to all that we've learned from postmodern theory without discarding concepts and metaphors that have been helpful to so many of us and to so many of our students" (Moore 2005, 202).

In some cases, institutional condonation of a student's "retention" of her "real voice" is theorized as an inclusionary mechanism for students who might otherwise feel alienated by academia. In other cases, the ability to articulate and distinguish between one's "own" voice and the voice of the institution are viewed as crucially empowering epistemological moves for students to feel academically capable.[15] In addition, some may believe that an important component of students' (especially young students') healthy psychological development includes a gradated process of moving from inner to outer voice, and that to short-circuit the valorization of a student's "own voice" in her writing would be to make developmentally and academically unrealistic demands of the student, or, worse still, to inflict possible long-lasting psychological damage.[16]

Some of the resilience of theoretically suspect models of voice in the composition classroom might be attributable, then, to teachers' reluctance to give up cherished composition commitments to student agency and social justice. How might one deploy a theoretically-informed understanding of voice without conceding composition's hard-fought advocacy of student agency, and without bolstering critiques of poststructuralism as relativist and apolitical? I will attempt to address this conundrum below.

VI. STRETCHING TENSIONS

Here is an example of an informal writing activity I assigned my first-year composition students in order to encourage them to play with and critically think about voice:

- Print out a sustained exchange that you have had on Facebook with one or more of your Facebook friends (for the purposes of this assignment, "sustained exchange" means an exchange where you posted three or more comments during an exchange based on one person's "status" post; the status post could be your own or someone else's)
- Now write 2–3 informal pages reflecting on your "voice" in the Facebook exchange you printed out—where does your voice come from? what characterizes it? is it consistent? is it similar to or different from the voices you use in other parts of your life (in class, for instance, or with your family)? use examples from the Facebook exchange to illustrate your points

When I asked students to write about the above question in my Fall 2011 first-year composition class, I was struck by the fact that a majority of the respondents (19 out of 22) in some way recognized that their Facebook "voices" were constructs.[17] They didn't say they were just "being themselves" or just writing in their "real" or "natural" voices. Some offered thoughtful theories on how these Facebook voices came to be developed, self-consciously elaborating on how art, craft, and learning create voice. For instance, Michael Shoar wrote, "I developed my 'voice' from years of being with friends who have Funny personalities" (Shoar 2011). For me, these recognitions are a helpful starting point for a discussion about academic writing and dismantling the commonplace that academic writing is less "real" or "natural" than any other type of writing, or that one voice is more genuine than another. One of my student respondents observed sagely, "there is a time and place for each different 'voice' I choose to carry out," suggesting a knowing understanding of how all voices are constructed and how their specific deployments can be strategic.

Now, I don't want to imply that all my first-year composition students were fully and seamlessly attuned to their poststructuralist selves. After all, even though they seemed to acknowledge the constructed nature of their non-academic (writing) voices, the majority of the respondents still explicitly or implicitly counterposed these voices against their "real" selves. One student suitably represented this point of view: "In the conversation that I had with my friend on Facebook, I noticed that I wasn't exactly being myself." So, the binary now posited all writing voices (fake) on one side, and the real self on the other. Whereas in the common student complaint against academic writing, academic voices are represented as contrary to one's real or natural voices, now it seems that all writing and all voices have moved to the same side of the opposition. While the modernist subject has hardly been dispensed with, at least the familiar opposition of "authentic" vs. "inauthentic" voice seems to have been at least temporarily forgotten. One student writer, in analyzing his Facebook post, commented, "My tone of voice here in this particular post is completely different from my voices i use in all other parts of my life" (Ringgold 2011). Note how this writer uses the plural "voices" to suggest how different voices come into play in different contexts in his life, and that he seems to see merely an array of voices, without necessarily privileging some over others or identifying some as being "truer" than others.

I assign this writing after we have defined and discussed voice in class, perhaps by referencing some student papers and published professional writing. An additional step could be added to the above assignment, asking students to comment on the voice they used to reflect on the Facebook exchange, comparing this voice with the original Facebook voice(s). The activity could also serve as a precursor to a more sustained formal assignment, autobiographical or not, addressing issues around voice. Because students begin the assignment by analyzing their Facebook voice(s), the assignment has by definition destabilized the assumption that students' Facebook voices are more real, more natural, or more authentic than their academic voices. The assignment also encourages students to define voice by looking at what constitutes voice through a close reading of their own text. This work of breaking down voice is the first step toward enabling students to (re)build, play with, refine, and refute voices.

One of the ways, then, that we might negotiate between the tensions I delineated in the previous section would be to emphasize the active construction of voice in writing, and to reflect on constructions of voice rather than to take voice as natural. We could ask student writers to consider the particular voice(s) they wish to use in a writing assignment, to reflect on the political and personal stakes in a particular voice, and to critically interrogate the available voice choices. We could provide students with strategies for distinguishing, evaluating, choosing, and articulating specific voices. We could encourage students to reflect on how these voices connect—or don't connect—to previous voices they have heard, read, imagined, and used in their own work. We could ask what social, cultural, and educational factors produced these previous voices, rather than what their "real" or "authentic" voice is and how they might go about cultivating such realness. This kind of emphasis would be theoretically and materially grounded in the sense that it would point to the rhetorical processes by which voices are constituted in texts and bodies of all kinds, rather than suggesting that a voice is just there, waiting to be discovered or articulated. But this emphasis could also allow for the role and responsibility of composer in the construction of voice. The ethical implications of positions advocated—and the strategies by which they are developed—would be no less important than if we were urging writers to find their true voices. In fact, one could say that writers are more responsible for voices they have constructed than for those that have simply found them or those they have unconsciously inhabited. And, certainly, to charge a writer with constructing a textual voice is not to assign any less agency to the writer than the paradigm that sees an effective writer as finding and expressing her "authentic voice." For writers who view their voice as marginalized, to learn the history and politics of this voice and to see its deployment as political intervention rather than uncontrollable inevitability can become the means to consciously construct and work on that voice, as experienced writers do.

I want to end this chapter with a caveat that returns to the question of intent raised in the previous chapter. As much as we might like to emphasize agency, ownership, and active authorship, we also need to recognize that writing often eludes an author's control. Moreover, we should not develop a theoretically-informed understanding of voice at the expense of falling into another humanist trap—privileging authorial intent as the apotheosis of textual meaning in the writing classroom. It would be ironic and hypocritical to reject essentialist, romantic views of voice en route to developing a more theoretically-robust composition pedagogy, only to resurrect epistemologies of the coherent humanist subject in the form of authorial intent in our eagerness to preserve student agency. So, an understanding of voice as actively constructed nevertheless needs to simultaneously attend to (and sometimes even value) the unexpected play of language and the meanings that writers can't control—not as obstacles to be revised away, but as inevitable complications of our constructions of voice, as additional dimensions of pleasure and danger in our texts. The masks of Freyer's *Ring* singers don't necessarily enable the performers to more carefully control what and where their voices do and go as much as they proliferate their increasingly enigmatic meanings and effects.

NOTES

1. For some discussions of the ways in which work done under the aegis of "multiculturalism" can serve to recenter dominant subjects by appropriating and ghettoizing the Other, see Barnard (2010), Villanueva (2009), and Worsham (1991). A growing body of recent scholarship (e.g., Mortimer-Sandilands and Erickson 2010) is also addressing constructions of nature and naturalness, building on earlier work by Raymond Williams (1980) and others.

2. For further discussion of the uses and abuses of discourses of cultural authenticity, see Barnard (2010).

3. Bowden (1999) provides a helpful history and critique of the metaphor of voice in composition. However, while my goal here is to discuss ways of using "voice" richly, productively, and in theoretically-informed ways, Bowden ultimately urges that voice be replaced by other metaphors. See also Vandenberg (1996) for an overview of the evolution of "voice" in composition.

4. For an overview of these arguments, see Bryant (2005) and Yancey (1994a).

5. Bryant is alluding to the Conference on College Composition and Communication (CCCC) 1974 "Students' Rights to Their Own Language" resolution. I want to avoid conflating voice with language; although the two concepts do intersect, their meanings differ. In addition, language is usually conceptualized socially and politically in composition studies, while voice is frequently understood as more individual and inwardly produced. Thus, discourses around language already carry some of the weight of the poststructuralist understandings of voice I am arguing for, though I also want to interrogate essentialist understandings of language as fixed and given.

6. For further critique of the uses and misuses of the "native informant," see Aneja (2005) and hooks (1994a).

7. Unlike contemporary composition textbooks, many handbooks do mention voice, but only in the technical context of explaining the differences between the grammatical use of active and passive voice.

8. See Lunsford and Lunsford (2008, especially 793) and Monroe (2009) for a discussion of the emphasis on academic rather than "personal" writing in contemporary composition pedagogy. However, the pendulum has already begun to swing back again, and we are currently seeing the reassertion of personal writing in composition scholarship and teaching (see, for example, Gottschalk 2011 and the special cluster of articles on personal writing in *College English* 64 [1] 2001).

9. See Baecker (2007) for a discussion of student/teacher perceptions of academic writing.

10. For a discussion of "free speech" in the context of liberal pluralism, see Barnard (2005).

11. See Royster (1996) for a general discussion of voice and subject position. See Moore (2005) for a nuanced defense of the concept of voice as politically important for marginalized subjects. hooks presents a compelling account of the political necessity of "coming to voice" for marginalized subjects, but also warns her readers about how racial biases can inform assumptions about "authentic voice" (hooks 1994d, 52).

12. See Bowden (2003) for further discussion of evolving (and even competing and contradictory) definitions of voice in composition. Brittenham and Hoeller (2004) also provide a generous and thoughtful definition of voice in *Key Words for Academic Writers*.

13. See Fish (2008) for a recent, polemical, and contested instance of the advocacy of this kind of pluralism in composition.

14. See Freisinger (1994) for an elaboration of this position.

15. For compelling arguments against the usual celebration of "code-switching" in composition and education, see Lu (2009) and Young (2009).

16. See Johnson (2011) for an innovative inter-subjective account of the psychological development of student writers. For another account of the relationship between writing and human development, see Herrington and Curtis (2000). Lanham (2007) argues against the privileging of "sincerity" in student writing, since most students haven't yet developed their "selves" (73, chapter 6). Lanham avoids the poststructuralist perspective that I favor.

17. In the following citations, I refer to students by name if they so requested. Student writers whose names are not given asked to remain anonymous.

5

ETHNOGRAPHY

In the opening sentence of their introduction to the anthology
Ethics and Representation in Qualitative Studies of Literacy, Kirsch
and Mortensen (1996b) were able to confidently assert that
"Qualitative approaches to research—ethnographies and case
studies in particular—continue to gain prominence in composition studies as researchers strive to enrich our understandings
of literacy in its myriad cultural context" (xix). Almost twenty
years later, the pace of ethnographic work and case studies in
composition scholarship has not slowed down, nor has the popularity of the pedagogical corollary to this scholarship waned,
meaning student-generated ethnographies as assignments in
university composition classes across the board, from first-year
composition courses to graduate seminars in rhetoric and composition.[1] In his chapter in the open access textbook, *Writing
Spaces: Readings on Writing, Volume 2*, Seth Kahn explains to students the importance and relevance of ethnography in composition classes: "Ethnographic writing challenges you to consider
everything that's interesting and difficult about writing" (Kahn
2011, 175). Ethnography as a genre, then, has become fairly
ubiquitous in composition scholarship and pedagogy, perhaps
betraying composition's desire to align itself with the social sciences and/or the field's part-origins in social science.

Another impetus toward ethnography certainly lies in composition's interests in issues around equity and social justice (see,
for example, Kahn 2011), community literacies, and investigat-
ing writing beyond the academy. This cluster of goals has been
articulated especially in discussions of service learning pedagogy. While service learning and ethnography are not coter-
minous, service learning courses often include ethnographic

DOI: 10.7330/9780874219470.c005

assignments and promote values, dispositions, and outcomes that can be implicit goals of ethnographic work. As Kelly Brotzman states in her explanation of the increasing popularity of service learning courses, universities "have become acutely aware that they need to address real-world problems and work toward the public good, lest they become irrelevant" (Brotzman 2011, 2). Cushman and Grabill (2008/09) outline some of the more specific permutations of this impetus:

> The historical roots that led to community literacy have also yielded shoots of growth in the areas of public rhetoric, cultural rhetoric, ethnography, research, and professional and technical communication. Central to all these areas is the fundamental understanding that writing matters; it can make a difference for peoples, organizations, and institutions. Depending on the purposes and exigencies for writing in these contexts, community-based writing can mobilize people, inform policy, seed new initiatives, draw audiences to events and forums, allow for greater participation in decision making, and make decision making transparent. (1)

For multiple reasons and as a result of interdisciplinary convergences, then, ethnography has become a composition commonplace. Its importance as a "commmonplace" in this book lies not only in its status as ethnography, but also in its intrication in ideologies of objectivity (the subject of chapter 7) and its use in projecting other composition values and practices.

At the same time ethnography was gaining ground in composition, it was losing ground in other disciplines, such as anthropology. Since the 1960s, challenges to conventional ethnography have included charges that its presumptions to objectivity (and, on a larger scale, its pretensions to being a "science") are fallacious; that its almost-inevitable origin in the West and frequent focus on non-Western Others reproduce ethnocentric biases; that the power relations between ethnographer and subject(s) reinforce existing social, cultural, and material inequities; and that its efforts to produce "knowledge" about the Third World collude in the imperialist project.[2] In 1988, Clifford Geertz articulated the conjunction between composition and ethnography that has fuelled my interest in this topic, and that marks the nexus of difficulty for composition: "What once seemed only technically difficult, getting 'their' lives into 'our' works, has turned morally, politically, even epistemologically delicate. . . . Indeed, the very right to write—to write ethnography—seems at risk" (Geertz 1988, 130).

However, as I illustrate in sections I-III below, we in composition don't yet have the strong tradition of anti-colonial critique of ethnographic models and methodologies that anthropology now has. So, what is the status of ethnography in composition scholarship and teaching? How has composition responded to, addressed, and incorporated postcolonial critiques of ethnography into its own ethnographic practices? And what is to be done with ethnography in composition?

I. COMPOSITION'S OWN REFLECTIONS ON ETHNOGRAPHY

Since composition by now has its own fairly long history of ethnographic work, I would be reluctant to cede ownership of ethnology to other disciplines like anthropology. Nevertheless, the challenges to ethnography have not been consistently incorporated into composition scholarship and courses since composition appropriated ethnography and took up its own ethnographic projects—which isn't to say that much work in anthropology and related disciplines doesn't still proceed with colonizing business as usual. Additionally, this isn't to say that more recent composition scholarship hasn't both participated in the critiques of ethnography that began before composition's adoption of ethnographic practices, as well as responded to these critiques by scrutinizing ethnographic practices in composition scholarship and pedagogy.[3] However, the transference of these theoretical critiques to ethnographic scholarship and teaching has been uneven.

In their introduction to a special issue of *Reflections* on service learning, Ellen Cushman and Jeffrey Grabill give a helpful overview of the history of service learning in composition, suggest some of the overlaps between service learning and ethnography, and discuss the role of ethnography in service learning and other community-based work. Tellingly, though, while Cushman and Grabill (2008/09) do cite some careful and critical ethnographies, the section of their introduction on "Ethnographies of Cultural Communities" includes no discussion of colonialism or the problematization of ethnography as a genre, discipline, and methodology. And, even among the many articles on service learning that do report on the problems encountered by instructors, students, and community partners in particular service learning courses (e.g., Cushman and Green 2010; Rumsey and Nihiser 2011), most tend to discuss the problems following a particular course's chronology on an ad hoc basis without any theoretical framing that refers to postcolonial theory or anticolonial critiques of the ethnographic project.

In their introduction to *Ethics and Representation in Qualitative Studies of Literacy*, Kirsch and Mortensen not only provide a welcome history of ethnographic work in composition and of critical reflection (or lack thereof) on ethnographic scholarship, but also gesture toward a broader theoretical framework for considering ethical issues in ethnographic methodology, including references to relevant feminist, postcolonial, and poststructuralist critiques of conventional ethnology (Kirsch and Mortensen 1996b, xxi). I envision my own work in this chapter as contributing to the conversations percolating in this anthology by deepening the theoretical critique of ethnography in composition, and by attempting to address the questions Kirsch and Mortensen raise in their introduction.

II. ETHNOGRAPHY IN COMPOSITION SCHOLARSHIP

I should note that—in addition to self-reflexive and critical ethnographic work in composition, such as those examples cited by Cushman and Grabill (2008/09) and one cited by Linda Brodkey (1996, 112) in *Writing Permitted In Designated Areas Only*—there are many scholars still producing conventional ethnographic work, apparently oblivious to the devastating and sustained critiques to which this kind of work has been subjected. I was surprised to discover, for instance, that at the 2003 Feminism(s) and Rhetoric(s) conference in Columbus, Ohio, keynote speaker Marcia Farr (2003) concluded her discussion of conversation patterns among a group of bi-national women moving between Chicago and Mexico by remarking on how moved she was with the project and how much she had become a part of the community she was studying: "a little bit of Mexico had forever become a part of me." The naiveté and condescension in this comment might suggest that it was a parody of stereotypically racist ethnographic work, were it not for the fact that the rest of Farr's talk was singularly unreflective on her methodologies, subjectivity, and relative position of power vis-à-vis her subjects.

Unreflective ethnographic practices can also infiltrate composition scholarship in more subtle forms, and, in some places, as integral components of modes and methodologies that are quite unique to composition. For instance, in the previous chapter I discussed the ways in which compositionists' citation practices when it comes to student sources often violate axiom 4: Students Are Writers. These practices also have particular resonances for ethnography. Frequently our own writing about our students and their work (though we often don't think of this as ethnography) uncritically reproduces some of the problematic traits of conventional ethnography. For example, the common practice in composition research of referring to real students by their first names only, or, still more troubling, by made-up names, echoes the hierarchies between subject and object in imperialist anthropology: the Others are anonymous, interchangeable, unindividualized, and, most importantly, their subjectivity can never match the authority of the writing subject. A case in point is Nancy Welch's (2002) *CCC* article, "'And Now That I Know Them': Composing Mutuality in a Service Learning Course." The article is exemplary in the author's articulation of the complex power relations between her students and their ethnographic subjects. However, Welch's own representation of her students is still very conventional. The opening paragraph of the piece introduces a quotation from one of her students:

"Shifting back and forth between present and past tense, Janis writes" (243). And the first footnote explains, "I've fictionalized the name of the community center as well as the names of the teens and staff [about whom the students wrote]. I draw on Janis's and Jacqui's writings with their permission" (261). The text offers no explanation for why students are referred to by first names only (in contrast to the other "professional" sources cited). Presumably "Janis" and "Jacqui" are the students' "real" names, since the author doesn't state otherwise (as she does with the names of the students' ethnographic subjects). Did the students request that the author use only their first names? Did the author assure them that only their first names would be used, as is the convention in composition scholarship? Was the use of first names a tool of reassurance to get the students to allow the author to quote their work? Was the impression given not only that this is the "way things are done," but also that this is somehow more desirable for the students, that this is for their benefit? The author never explains. Institutional Review Board (IRB) standards also have a role to play in these conventions—ironically, in mandating procedures to protect research subjects and assure their confidentiality. Such standards collude in patronizing student writers when they are constructed as research subjects rather than as "real" authors.

Of course, there are also examples of composition scholarship that resist the problematic kinds of student representation I have been discussing. For instance, in "Teaching the Rhetorical Possibilities of the Personal Essay," Janice Chernekoff (2003) cites her students by first and last names, parallel to her references to professional scholars, and gives full citation information for students' papers in her list of works cited. Her student sources are thus accorded the same degree of legitimacy (as writers and scholars) as her other sources. In *Standing in the Shadows of Giants*, Rebecca Moore Howard explicitly calls for students to be recognized as "authors" (Howard 1999, 137) and uses her students in her discussions of plagiarism, not merely to make a point about student writing, but as authoritative sources of opinion on the topic.

III. ETHNOGRAPHY IN COMPOSITION PEDAGOGY

As I have noted, the turn to ethnographic research in composition led more composition teachers to assign ethnographies in their classes. Consequently, the disjunctions multiplied. First, as the previous section suggests, while a new breed of "postmodern" ethnography is making its appearance in several disciplines, in many places the theory/praxis gap remains as wide as ever: traditional (uncritical) ethnographies continue to be produced (by compositionists and by scholars in other fields), and in some cases problematic ethnographic methodologies are reproduced uncritically as part of disciplinary conventions (e.g., standard references to student authors). These problems are then transferred to the pedagogical dissemination and implementation of ethnology.

Second, critical work on the use of ethnographies in pedagogical contexts doesn't match the work on ethnographic scholarship in quantity or theoretical scope. Thomas Trimble's (2008/09) essay in the service learning special issue of *Reflections* lists claims made for the value of ethnographic classroom assignments, while also recognizing that "ethnography continues to be problematized across the academy as both a research method and writing genre, due primarily to ongoing unease about both the politics and ethics of ethnographic representation. Ethnographic pedagogy, meanwhile, has received far less critical attention" (52). Trimble's point about the uneven theorization of problematic ethnographic practices in research compared to teaching is illustrated by the excellent Kirsch and Mortensen anthology mentioned above, in which most of the authors discuss their own work as scholars rather than as teachers. The authors of the foreword include graduate students who note how the book's chapters helped them to think through some of the dilemmas of the ethnographies they were working on as students, without elaborating on the specific results they achieved (Lunsford et al. 1996). Mary Sheridan's (2012) article "Making Ethnography Our Own," which considers how compositionists need to adapt ethnographic principles and practices to make them robust for our own field, focuses on Sheridan's own work and, by extension, the work of other scholars in composition, but does not address the ramifications of "the crises of representation" for composition pedagogy. This is not to fault Sheridan's article, but to point out where the focus of theorizing about ethnography in composition continues to lie. My hope is that the examples of student work in the latter sections of this chapter will help to flesh out the possibilities suggested by Trimble's and Sheridan's work.

A third disjunction, the theory-pedagogy gap I have been chronicling throughout this book, is exacerbated as the rush to pedagogies that include ethnography often results in the very types of ethnographic work that were being critiqued by scholars in composition and other disciplines. It has become quite fashionable for composition courses to include "ethnography" assignments in their curricula, but sometimes we are so thankful to receive a paper that is detailed and well-written that we forego challenging our students (and ourselves) to ask the bigger questions underlying the kind of work and writing involved in the assignment. And, then, in a predictably unfortunate chain of events, new composition textbooks hot on the heels of the ethnography fad often solidify pedagogies and assignments that seem oblivious of the history of "anti-ethnography." For example, the 2004 composition reader, *Exploring Literacy*, includes a section on "Writing in Ethnographic Genres" that rehearses the most conventional of ethnographic epistemologies and methodologies, and which uses as a model essay an uncritical 1975 article that, in turn, acknowledges its debt to a "classic article" from 1964 (Kutz 2004, 250). The 1980s and 1990s seem to be forgotten by the book's editor, and the book fails to grapple with the more complex and contested understanding of ethnography we have today (something that even revised editions of Margaret Mead's (2001) now "classic" ethnography, *Coming of Age in Samoa*, routinely address in the preface). In its prompts for possible writing assignments, *Exploring Literacy* instructs student writers to use their ethnographic observations "to give as rich a picture as possible of community life," and urges them to "bring out the larger patterns of meaning" they have found in the communities that are the subject of their ethnographic research (Kutz 2004, 279). Nowhere does the assignment question the accuracy or efficacy of the ethnographer's supposedly omniscient gaze, nor the ethnographer's moral right to construct the "meaning" of a community based on a few hours of observation.

However, critiques of ethnography are making their way into some pedagogical materials. For instance, Kahn's chapter on ethnographic writing in *Writing Spaces: Readings on Writing* provides students with more nuanced advice than *Exploring Literacy* does, and Kahn devotes substantial space in the chapter to discussing the ethics of representation. However, his admonition to students to heed "the responsibility to our participants to ensure that what we say about them is fair, reasonable, and accurate" (Kahn 2011, 178) ultimately skirts the central issues of representation, power, and objectivity by assuming we address the problems with ethnography by just trying harder within the framework of the strategies and assumptions that themselves have been called into question. "Accuracy" is still constructed as a desirable and possible goal, as if the student ethnographer were merely writing down "fact." To be fair to Kahn, I should point out that he does elsewhere in the chapter note the impossibility of objectivity, and he also emphasizes "reciprocity" as key component of ethical ethnographic work (though the concept is left fairly unproblematized, with no discussion of how the power relations between ethnographer and ethnographic subject, including the contexts that create and enable these subject positions, might circumscribe and inflect such "reciprocity"). The fourth edition of *Fieldworking: Reading and Writing Research*, an entire textbook devoted to "fieldwork" (and offered as a text for a variety of disciplines, including composition), also articulates a relatively thoughtful and critical approach to ethnography. The authors caution students against "**colonization**" (Sunstein and Chiseri-Strater 2012, 4, emphasis original) and note the importance of reflection in ethnographic work "because, in the end, every fieldstudy is also about the self" (52).

But these more self-reflexive and critical pedagogical approaches still seem to be the exception rather than the norm. After noting the relatively low level of critical theorization on ethnographcially-focused pedagogy, Trimble (2008/09) goes on to discuss the ethnographies that his students produced as part of a service learning course. Although the strategies the student ethnographers use implicitly address some of the problems associated with ethnographic work in general, Trimble doesn't explicitly discuss the specific problems of the "politics and ethics of ethnographic representation," or how to situate student work in the context of and in response to these politics. I hope that my own work in the following sections of this chapter can move beyond Trimble's catalog to specifically unpack critical ethnographic methodologies in the contexts of postcolonial and anti-colonial politics, as well as student projects originating in composition classrooms.

IV. ANTI-ETHNOGRAPHY?

My aim in the preceding sections is not to demonize particular scholars or texts, but rather to point to representative instances of common practices in composition scholarship and textbooks where we can see the theory/praxis gaps I have been charting in this book, and to develop a heuristic to problematize my representation of my own students in this chapter. As I discussed with my students how I might best represent them in my research, we were faced with several dilemmas. If I am to avoid speaking for them, should I merely quote them precisely? But aren't quotes inevitably manipulated to suit the quoter's agenda, and wouldn't my quoting of them still result in the same kind of appropriation of their voices as my speaking for them would? What about having my students as co-authors of this text? To what extent would they be able to exert control over the text and its reception, given academic hierarchies' overdetermination of the etiquette undergirding scholarly writing, and given my position in these hierarchies and my knowledge of these conventions? There are no clear-cut solutions to these problematics; the recognition of this indeterminacy, however, can become a productive pedagogical tool for unsettling students' and teachers' desires for quick fixes or definitive answers.

My own attempts to intersect ethnographic theory with pedagogical practice began with a writing course I developed for students in the social sciences, focusing on the question of how we should represent Others. This course was part of an innovative program of advanced writing courses required of students at the university where I was teaching at the time. All students are required to complete an expository writing course beyond their first-year composition course, and are given courses to choose from that are either discipline-specific (law, engineering, etc.) or that group disciplines together under broader categories (e.g., arts and humanities). I decided to develop my social science course around the issue of ethnographic representation, since this has become one of the central ethical concerns impacting many disciplines and areas within the social sciences (and elsewhere), including gerontology, anthropology, ethnography, history, political science, social work, psychology, journalism, international relations, marketing, advertising, linguistics, education, women's studies, queer theory, disability studies, postcolonial studies, and ethnic studies. Of added importance to me as a compositionist, I viewed the question of ethnographic representation as a writing issue, since so many of these representations of the Other take the form of written texts, and since ethnographic assignments have now become commonplace in composition.

It was my hope that students find the work of engaging with important questions around representation intellectually challenging and stimulating, as well as a lot of fun, and that this work would complicate and enrich their sense of self as writers and participants in the social sciences. We began the course by reading and writing about the now well-established charge that representations of the Other employ imperialist methodologies and epistemologies. We examined Mead's (2001) *Coming of Age in Samoa* through multiple rhetorical and political lenses, as a liminal text that broke new ethnographic ground, but that also embodies some of the problems with ethnography. Students then chose any representation of the Other (in any medium) to analyze, and the course ended by inviting students to create their own anti-imperialist mini-ethnographies, or, as I sometimes call them, "anti-ethnographies," since this project not only embodied students' careful chronicling and analysis of their ethnographic subjects, but also demonstrated their awareness of the difficulties and problems associated with writing about the Other, and their attempts to engage with and overcome these problems.

The last assignment was, needless to say, quite challenging. Some students found it paralyzing. By this point in the course, they had developed a fairly sophisticated critique of ethnographic methodologies and epistemologies, and had realized that there are no easy solutions to the problems. They readily acknowledged that ethnocentric bias undermines the scientific claims of much ethnography, but they also recognized, though often with regret, that bias is inevitable—so, to counter the problems with conventional ethnography by simply saying "I will write an unbiased ethnography" in fact creates more problems than it solves. Given that some postcolonial cultural critics (e.g., Trinh T. Minh-ha 1989) have suggested that anthropology as a discipline is, by definition, imperialist, aren't we setting ourselves up for inevitable failure as soon as we engage with this assignment? Shouldn't anthropology just be abolished in toto? Given the seemingly exponentially increasing problems with the ethnographic project, why engage in ethnography (or this course) at all? As the authors of the foreword to *Ethics and Representation in Qualitative Studies of Literacy* ask, "If the project of research is so fraught with dangers of misrepresentation, appropriation, and violence, why not just give up the enterprise entirely?" (Lunsford et al. 1996, xiv).

My response is that, first, ethnography will continue whether we want it to or not, and whether we like the ethnographic work that is being done or not. I would rather my students (and others) crtically intervene in the ethnographic enterprise than allow it to proceed unchallenged because their interventions might be problematic. Second, I am not entirely convinced that ethnography as a discipline should be done away with; while the knowledges it produces in the context of Western representations of the Other are seldom completely benign,[4] to abandon any efforts to learn about other cultures would doom the West to more of the kinds of ignorance and arrogance that the critiques of ethnography make painfully apparent. Third, I believe that the issues raised by the questions surrounding ethnography are interesting and important in and of themselves, and worthy of engaging because of their implications for knowledge, representation, and writing in general. Even if my students ultimately come to the conclusion that ethnography should be abandoned, the process by which they come to this conclusion provides valuable opportunities for reflection on concerns pertinent to a host of disciplines and media, including writing.

How, then, to address the political, intellectual, and moral objections that have been made to the ethnographic project? Since the ethnographic gaze so often looks unidirectionally from First to Third World, from power to powerless, wouldn't it behoove ethnographers to study the sources of power, rather than the subjects on whom that power is exercised? As Ralph Cintron puts it, "Metaphorically speaking, for every hour spent among the vulnerable, an hour needs to be spent in those sites that are, in part, responsible or complicit in the making of vulnerability" (Cintron 2002, 940). However, while the political imperative of Cintron's injunction is laudable, it also risks recapitulating some of the problems that critical ethnography seeks to redress: seeing the Other only as a function of/in terms of the dominant subject, and returning the focus to the seats of power, when one of the purposes of ethnography is precisely to shift that focus in order to expand the researcher's and reader's horizons/understandings/sympathies. We can take Cintron's demand a step further: if, as some critics insist, anthropologists should avoid the power hierarchies and exoticizing impulses that inevitably accompany representations of the Other by studying their own cultures, shouldn't we all just write about ourselves (the "autoethnography" assignments that are so popular in composition classes)? Wouldn't such an imperative foster the same kind of insular ethnocentrism that the abolition of ethnography might enable? And wouldn't it, as Linda Alcoff argues, act as a cover for the failure to engage in political activism? Alcoff writes,

> But a retreat from speaking for [others] will not result in an increase in receptive listening in all cases; it may result merely in a retreat into a narcissistic yuppie lifestyle in which a privileged person takes no responsibility whatsoever for her society. She may even feel justified in exploiting her privileged capacity for personal happiness at the expense of others on the grounds that she has no alternative.
>
> The major problem with such a retreat is that it significantly undercuts the possibility of political effectivity. There are numerous examples of the practice of speaking for others that have been politically efficacious in advancing the needs of those spoken for, from Rigoberto Menchu to Edward Said and Steven Biko. . . . The point is not that for some speakers the danger of speaking for others does not arise, but that in some cases certain political effects can be garnered in no other way. (Alcoff 1995, 107)

Self-reflection on the part of the ethnographer has also been offered as a way to forestall uncritical assumptions of neutrality, but this, too, could be an easy and unsatisfactory flight from a much more complex problem: often writers—who are now aware of the critiques of ethnography—preface their work with a fashionable discussion of their methodology and location (class, race, gender, nationality, etc.), but then proceed as before; the self-reflexivity doesn't impact the ensuing ethnographic account, except inasmuch as it gives the writers the self-satisfaction of thinking they have produced a "hip" ethnography. Bruce Horner notes this call for self-reflexivity from professional ethnographers: "precisely because they point to an ideal of academic professionalism, such calls tend to obscure the material social conditions of ethnographic work. As a result, what is intended as a cautionary practice can become a textually commodified guarantor of professional purity" (Horner 2002, 576). Linda Brodkey points out how quickly an ethnographer's identification of her narrative stance can give way to

an "ethnographic present," from which the narrator has dis-
appeared (Brodkey 1996, 110). In the case of student writers,
then, it is not so much that self-reflexivity is used to gain professional mileage, but that it can, as with the case of the professionals, work to foreclose any further engagement with the
problematics of ethnography—"We've covered that." A second
problem with this type of meta-reflection on the ethnographic
process is the possibility that the ethnographer becomes so
taken up with this self-reflexivity that she becomes completely
self-absorbed, producing an ethnography only about herself
(a charge directed at Trinh (1982) in response to her ground-
breaking documentary film, *Reassemblage*).

Of course, my students rose to the challenge of creating the
seemingly impossible critical ethnographies that my final assignment required. They used various multimedia technologies to
reconceptualize the relationships among ethnographer, ethnographic subject, and their readers. In developing a variety of
research and rhetorical strategies to document their subjects in
inventive ways, the students sometimes produced more thoughtful ethnographies than those published by professionals in the
field. My students' rhetorical strategies included having their
ethnographic subjects write about their ethnographers as a way
of suggesting that the ethnographer should be an object of scru-
tiny as much as her subjects; asking their subjects to interview
one another in an attempt to circumvent the problematic power
dynamics inherent in the ethnographer-subject relationship;
inserting all kinds of self-reflexive and other interventions into
their ethnographies in order to interrogate their own ethnographies while they created them (not unlike the "interruptive"
techniques praised by Brodkey (1996, 112)); and even creating
fictitious ethnographies as a commentary on the manipulations
and fictions that necessarily characterize all ethnographies, and
as a satire of the reader's will to know the "truth" about the ethnographic subject, or the reader's delusion that she is learning
this truth through reading ethnography.

In one particularly ambitious multimedia project, Elizabeth
Burkholder (2003) created a complex series of frames to

contextualize and complicate her work. Burkholder's Power-Point used photographs and text to "document" the school lives of a group of special education students she had been working with at a local public school. The piece began with an introduction that outlined the author's goals for the work and retrospective insights on reviewing the project, then displayed the photographs, each one containing a substantial narrative commentary that included a discussion of the process of taking the photograph (some photographs were accompanied by two pieces of commentary). The photographs were followed by a section entitled "Photographer's Choices," in which the author discussed her photographic method and techniques—and the rationale for them—as a way of demystifying the final products. The next section, "My experiences," provided a narrative account of how the author came to undertake the project and the mundanities of its day to day execution, and was followed by a "Conclusion," a section entitled "Notes looking back," and, finally, a section labeled "My failures." Among the many strategies Burkholder used to fulfill the assignment's charge to address and embody critiques of ethnography, she resisted the urge to deludedly suggest that her time with her subjects made her "one of them" by repeatedly drawing attention to her outsider status and acknowledging her biases rather than trying to efface her presence (for instance, in the caption for the first photograph, she emphasized her subjectivity with the phrase, "This is one of my favorite photos"). In her "Conclusion," Burkholder even responded to Alcoff's concern about self-reflexive ethnographic work evacuating the political from its agendas by situating her project as an intervention into current social and political efforts to revise protocols for special education students in California public schools. In the "My failures" section, she established her project as a moment in an ongoing process, rather than as a finished and finite body of knowledge, by pointing out its flaws and offering suggestions on how future work could be improved.

In the self-evaluations the students turned in with their mini-ethnographies, they often reflected on the agonizing decisions they had to make or defer, even explicitly offering their own work as critiques of other writing in the field. Kelly Fitzgerald, for instance, whose mini-ethnography profiled a group of women living in a shelter for homeless women—whom she taught as part of a service learning course at the university—reflected,

> I think the biggest strength of my paper is the way in which I included the women's handwriting in my paper. . . . I think it would be great for the *LA Times* to publish several papers/ stories/articles written on volunteers and their experiences just like I have—all the stories I have read are written in the point of view of the volunteer and include only very little info. on the person or group of people who are receiving the service. (Fitzgerald 2003)

While Fitzgerald's incorporation of her subjects' handwriting into her ethnography might be more problematically appropriative than she suggests, she does destabilize the subject-object relation in her project in two ways. First, she questions her own ethnographic authority: "At times, I have been frustrated by my inability to make a difference in the lives of these women. I admit that sometimes I do not know all the answers. I often wonder if there is someone more qualified that could help these women—I'm just a student!" A second transgressive component to Fitzgerald's ethnography revolves around a discussion she and I had about the project, and her reflection on why she was so interested in writing about these women in the first place: she realized that a relative's homelessness many years ago had subconsciously compelled her work on this assignment. I urged her to write about this in the ethnography itself, which she agreed to do. Ultimately, she turned the ethnographic gaze upon herself.

Another student, who requested that I not cite him by name, wrote his ethnography in the form of two voices, with the second voice critiquing the first one as a running commentary throughout. He discussed the implications of this strategy for readers in his self-evaluation of the paper:

> I think my main strength is my critique of my paper as my paper progresses. I tried to provide counterarguments to encourage

the reader to challenge my views. The idea of encouraging the
reader to disagree with me came to me while I was reading a
letter from Michael Moore on common[dreams].org. He wrote
that we should not be afraid to disagree or speak up. He uses his
Oscar speech as an example.

By actually providing readers with a model by which to critique
the author, this writer took Fitzgerald's questioning of her own
authority a step further. Such a degree of reader-author inter-
action, and the radical provisionality of authorial authority, is
unheard of in conventional ethnographic writing. In what I
would argue is an equally subversive conceptualization of ethnography, another student, who also requested to remain anonymous, wrote of his ethnography, "A high degree of subjectivity
is intended, the inherent drawbacks of presenting the Other as
an outsider are meant to be obvious. I question myself during
the paper as I questioned myself thinking about the subject."
To say that subjectivity is inevitable is one thing, but to imagine
deploying one's subjectivity in order to draw attention to the
limitations of the ethnographic project fundamentally rede-
fines the purpose and status of ethnography. Here, subjectivity,
rather than a regrettable inevitability, is conceptualized as a tool
deployed to foreground the constructions of the text/author
and critique the ethnographic project. Ethnography becomes
its own critique.

V. (PRODUCTIVE) UNSETTLINGS

I don't want to posit my students' work as unproblematic, or
present my course as a utopian political solution to the composition commonplace of ethnography or the vexing questions
around representation in general. Surely the student work
I have cited can be critiqued on various grounds. Certainly,
many disappointing papers were written in the course—many
students reverted to rehearsing the disciplinary, professional,
pedagogical, social, and political axioms they were taught and
felt comfortable with—and I have struggled with the complexities and contradictions of the material, as well as with my own

discomfort with my changing definitions and understandings of the terms we treat.

Because this work, to a large extent, ventures into "uncharted territory," it has also prodded me into revising my paradigms of writing, teaching, and evaluation. Often, I have found my own assumptions about student writing, and my own teacherly authority, challenged and enriched. On one memorable occasion, I came to a whole-class writing workshop feeling confident that the student text under discussion, a collaborative critical ethnography about visitors to a local bar, lacked a "point" and needed more commentary from the authors. Each of the female and male co-writers described the same interactions among the bar-goers, but these interactions seemed routine to me, and the differences in the descriptions lacking significance. I listened to other class members talk about the piece's complexity and subtlety, the possibility that the differences between the two writers' perspectives might be explained in terms of gender, the equally plausible possibility that the differences in perspective had nothing to do with gender, and the even more interesting possibility that both kinds of "differences" might well be the construction of the readers. As a result of this discussion, I completely altered my opinion, and confessed to the class that I had done so. I started to think of the piece as being as much about reading and the readers as it was about the writers and their subjects. I now valued the elliptical elements in the project, and thought of its lack of explicit focus as a strength rather than a failing. Other dilemmas and reversals plagued me. I even found myself worrying over exactly what constituted an "ethnography," since our dissections of the genre had made its boundaries so fuzzy that anything—or nothing—could be included in that category.

In retrospect, I see these pedagogical and intellectual crises as formative components of the projects we were all (teacher and students) undertaking, rather than as impediments to the smooth running of syllabi and assignments, or as reasons to abandon the work or teaching of ethnography. I believe that one of the values of this work with ethnography, for students and teachers, lies precisely in its grappling with these problems of definition and representation, in students and teachers experiencing the ways in which writing—how they write something, and how they conceptualize writing about something—shapes meaning and understanding for them, their readers, and the subjects of their discourse.

These are not esoteric questions. A quick survey of US media and political representations of Iraqis preceding the US's 2003 invasion of Iraq, or of Muslims post-9/11 (and continuing today), is ample evidence of one possible set of formative consequences of ethnographic writing—in this case, a horrifically reimagined ethnocentric arrogance and imperialist violence. A pedagogy that situates ethnographic projects in the context of these media representations and their political deployments enables students not only to realize the political relevance of their academic study of ethnography, but also to see the connections between writing and action, fulfilling one of the initial impetuses for ethnographic work in composition that I alluded to at the beginning of this chapter. These understandings of the material impact of ethnographic writing, in turn, inform students' reading of and participation in writing in their disciplines, as well as in their larger social and political contexts. Once students realize the extent to which representations of the Other enform material reality, their own rhetorical work takes on added urgency. This, of course, is also a challenge to compositionists, writing teachers, and teachers in other disciplines, to intervene into the ethnographic project as it is variously manifested in our cultures and curricula, and to conceptualize this intervention as much a question of writing as it is a question of history, politics, and sociality.

NOTES

1.   Wendy Bishop's (1999) history of ethnographic writing research noted that significant numbers of composition scholars moved to ethnographic approaches in the 1980s and 1990s (12–15). See Sheridan (2012) for an additional history of ethnography in composition.

2.   Some of the now classic critiques of ethnography (though the degree of investment in conventional methodologies and epistemologies differs widely) include Clifford (1988), Clifford and Marcus (1986), Geertz (1988), Hymes (1999), and Marcus and Fischer (1999). Kahn (2011) gives a concise overview of ethnography's colonialist origins. Kurt Spellmeyer (1993, especially chapter 8) makes some interesting parallels between composition and anthropology, mostly unflattering to the former. However, Spellmeyer is interested in showing where composition as a field has not yet gone, rather than in specifically discussing ethnographic practices in composition.

3.   For examples of such work in composition scholarship, including representative recent scholarship on service learning in the context of composition studies and a discussion of problems around service learning, see Brodkey (1996, 106ff.), Brotzman (2011), Brown (2004), Cintron (2002), Cushman and Green (2010), Himley (2004), Horner (2002), Kirklighter et al. (1997), Rumsey and Nihiser (2011), and Welch (2002). Brown's article begins with a helpful summary of the critiques of ethnography, then goes on to critique the critiques. While Himley's essay does not provide any answers to the critiques, it does give an articulate overview of the problems of representation in the context of service learning. For an overview of recent scholarship on issues in service learning, see Remley (2012).

4.   See Edward Said (1979) for one account of how imperialism puts to use supposedly disinterested scholarly production about the Other. The work of Said (1979, 1989) and Noam Chomsky (1987) has consistently chronicled the (sometimes unwitting) collusions between Western academia and Western imperialism.

6
AUDIENCE

The recent reenergized attention to audience in composition scholarship and teaching supposedly signals attempts to honor students as writers (axiom 4), who don't just dutifully compose for their teachers.[1] But, as I suggested in chapter 3, this imperative breaks down in the face of more entrenched pedagogical procedures and writerly dispositions associated with the process movement in composition. In this chapter, I am interested in thinking more specifically through the ways in which notions of audience are constructed in composition, especially composition textbooks and pedagogy. However, the injunction about audience awareness is not exactly the commonplace I wish to tackle here. Neither will I follow the venerable line of scholarship that has engaged in a nuanced and theoretically-informed scholarly discussion of when and how audiences do and should get constructed by writers, particularly student writers (e.g., Ede and Lunsford 1984; Elbow 1987). Rather, my goal is to interrogate common ways in which students are explicitly and implicitly instructed to shape their writing according to imputed audience demands, especially in what is termed academic writing, argumentative writing, persuasive writing, and academic essays (genres that, as I note in chapter 4, have come to find special favor in the composition classroom in the last thirty years, in the wake of some disaffection with expressivism and disdain for personal narrative).

The relative stability and reductiveness of instructions to composition students about how audience considerations should inform their writing is especially surprising and disheartening, given the generous and flexible ways in which scholars (and, on their heels, textbooks) are now treating persuasion, argument,

DOI: 10.7330/9780874219470.c006

and essays per se. Audience as a commonplace, then, speaks to a particular, narrow, and problematic notion of audience that is constructed in composition: the "general audience" that students are supposed to write for. As I adumbrate below, though, this commonplace is also important insofar as it is intricated in reductive understandings of writing strategies, forms, and genres such as essay, argument, and persuasion. In addition, and more significantly, this audience imperative is implicated in creating and enforcing bourgeois and other politically inflected conceptualizations and parameters of discourse and civility, and thus can be seen as advancing the idea of composition as a space for teaching students how to accommodate themselves to corporate capitalism, an accommodation that Richard Ohmann (1976) described so contemptuously (and presciently) in *English in America.*

I. EXPANSIVE FORMS

I want to contextualize my discussion of audience by briefly tracing what I see as opposing trends in constructions of composition and composition pedagogy. On the one hand, efforts to rehabilitate the essay form and broaden our conceptions of argument have invited flexible understandings of common composition genres and rhetorical strategies. Yet, on the other hand, understandings, explanations, and constructions of audience have not undergone similar interrogations, broadenings, and multiplications.

In *Common Ground: Dialogue, Understanding, and the Teaching of Composition*, Kurt Spellmeyer (1993), urging a conceptualization of writing as a "transgressive movement from 'knowledge' to knowing," comments exasperatedly on what the essay as a form has been reduced to in much composition pedagogy: "I can think of no genre, however, less conducive to such a movement than the rigidly formal, conceptually straitened 'freshman theme,' which prevents in almost every writer's case the occurrence of what the *historical essay*—the dialogical, open-ended essay—permits and even celebrates: an event of language, a transforming of the writer's conceptual horizon" (22). Spellmeyer hints at what gets lost in the drive for linearity when the essay is reduced to the pro/con argument so ubiquitous in first-year composition, often resulting in simplistic argument papers that feel the need to line everything up according to a thesis, at the cost of jettisoning, co-opting, or bulldozing over complexity and multiplicity. Narrow, thesis-driven expository writing can also negatively impact one's engagement with secondary sources. For student writers, in particular, the imperative to mine sources for quotes[2] in order to "support" a predictable position on one of a standard set of topics often results in little engagement with these sources, and little discovery, revelation, or pleasure in reading or writing.

Spellmeyer's observation also points to efforts (by scholars, at least) to move the essay back to the more open-ended raison d'être of its historical roots. William Zeiger argues, for instance, that Montaigne's "Essaies" follow the original meaning of "essay" as a trial or experiment (Zeiger 1985, 454–56), avoiding assertive conclusions and demonstrating the value of exploring ideas for their own sake. According to Zeiger, school children during Montaigne's time also wrote such exploratory essays, and Montaigne's rhetoric was actually more in keeping with Aristotelian traditions than today's constructions of Aristotle in many composition classrooms: "The domination of the composition class by the expository essay represents a temporary victory of the art of demonstration, the modern way of 'proving,' over the older way of 'proving,' the art of inquiry." Christy Wampole (2013) follows suit in embracing the essay form in a *New York Times* article, referencing Montaigne and arguing that the essay provides "an alternative to the dogmatic thinking that dominates much of social and political life in contemporary America," but that "Much of the writing encountered today that is labeled as 'essay' or 'essay-like' is anything but." William Covino is interested in wresting classical rhetoric more generally away from its hegemonic appropriations by composition, arguing that the major figures of classical rhetoric "define and demonstrate rhetoric as the elaboration of ambiguity" (Covino

1988a, 2, 9). Covino celebrates those rhetors who embody rhetoric as "an art of wondering, and writing as a mode of *avoiding* rather than *intending* closure."[3]

I have noticed the potential of Zeiger's and Covino's preferred models firsthand at CSUN, where the recent adoption of a new first-year writing curriculum that "postponed" argument in order to allow students to play with, explore, and develop ideas first encouraged my students to create more rigorous and intellectually satisfying papers, instead of the formulaic pro/con arguments that were the staple of our previous curriculum. The problem, though (besides faculty members who were resistant to assigning anything other than "argument essays"), is that "argument" is still positioned and privileged as the pinnacle toward which students are working in the final paper of the assignment sequence. Exploration itself then becomes co-opted in the service of an argument essay that is supposed to form the culminating assignment of the course.

Today, argument has become so synonymous with college composition that the Bedford/St. Martin's catalog for textbooks in composition, "developmental English," and literature now includes an entire section titled "Argument Texts and Readers" in the composition section, including texts with titles such as *From Critical Thinking to Argument, Practical Argument, Contemporary and Classical Arguments, Argument Simplified, The Elements of Argument, The Structure of Argument,* and, of course, *Everything's an Argument* (Bedford/St. Martin's 2010). The textbook *Current Issues and Enduring Questions* is advertised with the blurb "All you need to teach argument" (31). Argument itself, though, is conceptualized relatively flexibly, perhaps as a way of inviting varied types of student writing, or as a reaction against its dominance as part of the baggage of the recent privileging of academic writing that I traced in chapter 4, and possibly in deference to some of the critiques of the agonistic tone and reductive method that had come to characterize conceptualizations of argument in first-year composition.[4] The textbook *Elements of Argument,* for instance, begins by reassuring students, "Of course, not all arguments end in clear victories for one side or another. Nor should they" (Rottenberg and Winchell 2012, 3). *The Craft of Argument* follows suit: "The image of argument as close combat is encouraged by our language . . . But forget the battles" (Williams et al. 2003, 3). And the expansive catalog of argument in *Everything's an Argument* includes "Arguments to Meditate or Pray" and "Arguments to Explore" (Lunsford and Ruszkiewicz 2013).[5]

Agonism itself has been defended and nuanced. An instructive case in point is Patricia Roberts-Miller's defense of agonism via an analysis of Hannah Arendt's rhetoric. Roberts-Miller argues that Arendt's "polemical agonism" is a function of her critique of totalitarianism, and that Arendt makes the strongest argument "if not for agonism, then at least for replacing much of our dislike of conflict with a mistrust of consensus" (Roberts-Miller 2002, 587). In her discussion of Arendt, Roberts-Miller makes a distinction between persuasion and what she sees as Arendt's "polemical agonism": "In polemical agonism, however, one's intention is not necessarily to prove one's case, but to make public one's thought in order to test it . . . In persuasive agonism, success is achieved through persuasion; in polemical agonism, success may be marked through the quality of subsequent controversy" (595). Roberts-Miller's gloss of Arendt here points to some of the possibilities of conceptualizing audience that move beyond the need to persuade the standard "skeptical audience" often demanded for conventional argument papers, as I discuss below.

II. THE GENERAL AUDIENCE

The third edition of the composition textbook *The Informed Argument* includes the now obligatory insistence that "Argumentation demands a clear sense of audience" (R. Miller 1992, 4), but this opening openness (many different kinds of audience seem possible) is quickly narrowed in the following paragraph: "In written argumentation, it is usually best to envision an audience that is skeptical" (4). This advice—and related admonitions and exhortations around and about measured tone, counterarguments, logic, and certain types of evidence—explicitly or implicitly inform much of the teaching and writing that happens in composition classrooms, and undergird the textbooks that often propel this teaching and writing. Phrases like "anticipating counterarguments" often function as the preferred jargon for this commonplace in composition pedagogy, especially when students are assigned those ubiquitous "argument essays." For instance, the second edition of the textbook *They Say/I Say* includes "consider opposing arguments" in its list of requirements of "critical thinking and writing," and the book explicitly includes, among its templates designed to help composition students use secondary sources effectively, one "for entertaining a counterargument" (Graff and Birkenstein 2010, 2, xxi).

Even some textbooks and scholarship that champion "alternative" and/or subaltern rhetorics and subjects still end up making the persuasion of potentially hostile audiences the goal of these rhetorics. For instance, one could argue that while John Schilb's (2007) recent book *Rhetorical Refusals: Defying Audiences' Expectations* chronicles rhetorical moves that might defy conventional composition wisdom, these moves are nevertheless designed, as James Porter insists, not to dismiss the audience, "but with the intent to persuade" (Porter 2008, 810). As Schilb himself argues in his opening definition of the term "rhetorical refusal," "I use rhetorical refusal to denote an act of writing or speaking in which the rhetor pointedly refuses to do what the audience considers rhetorically normal. By rejecting a procedure that the audience expects, *the rhetor seeks the audience's assent* to another principle, cast as a higher priority" (Schilb 2007, 3, my emphasis). Thus, Schilb argues that Adrienne Rich's refusal of the National Medal for the Arts in 1997 was designed to "prod the federal government to share her priorities" (7). In every case Schilb treats in *Rhetorical Refusals*, the apparent disregard for one's audience and the protocols of discursive reciprocity masks a fervent desire to engage and persuade putatively hostile listeners/readers.

Of course, there are exceptions. The textbook *From Inquiry to Argument*, for example, recognizes that an intended audience might be "allied" with the writer, and lays out differentiated hierarchies of rhetorical appeals that writers might use in writing for "supportive," "hostile," or "mixed or neutral" audiences (McMeniman 1999, 15–16). These possibilities encourage writing that has a variety of functions, and that can refuse hegemonic audience normalizations, as I explain in sections III and IV below.

What's wrong with the commonplaces around the general audience I have described? I certainly see value in "entertaining counterargument," but I have a problem with this aphorism becoming a sine qua non for *all* academic writing that composition students produce, for the reasons I explain below. As with the clarity injunction I discussed in chapter 2, a required consideration of alternative viewpoints might seem commonsensical, but it masks a far-reaching embroilment in ideology and power relations that this commonsensicalness belies.

Besides the more generic poststructuralist, postcolonial, feminist, and other critiques of universalism itself, which I will discuss further in chapter 7, the conjuring of a putatively hostile but potentially persuadable reader carries more specific ideological baggage. In *Seductive Reasoning: Pluralism as the Problematic of Contemporary Literary Theory*, Ellen Rooney (1989) argues that, in the arena of literary theory, any attempt at persuasion constitutes an appeal to liberal pluralism. According to Rooney, pluralism is based "on the theoretical possibility of universal or general persuasion," and "the pluralist's invitation to critics and theorists of all kinds to join him in 'dialogue' is a seductive gesture that constitutes every interpreter—*no matter what her conscious critical affiliation*—as an effect of the desire to persuade" (1–2). Rooney unpacks the attempt at "general persuasion" as a liberal pluralist erasure of difference in the assumption that all readers are equally amenable to persuasion by a sufficiently skillful argument. This argument seems especially applicable to composition studies and pedagogy, or to the ways in which the imperative to appeal to a mythical "man on the street" denies the particular interests and stakes that specific individuals and communities might have in certain critical positions and practices, and thus enforces hegemonic political ideologies as it posits the existing political machinery of liberalism as adequate to fulfill the needs and desires of all, and its subjects as universal and uniform liberals. The denial of difference is always a denial of an Other. If one believes that one's "theory" or claim can and will (after argument and analysis) appeal to "everyone" (a little something for everyone), one assumes that no conflict is significant enough to create irreconcilable differences. Only those already in positions of privilege can afford to entertain such a bland sense of opposition: conflict must be "resolved" without upsetting the existing order. This means that conflicting viewpoints have to be accommodated by and contained within liberalism, even those viewpoints that challenge liberalism. This is an important point to make, beyond the many other arguments for not imagining writing as an attempt to persuade a hostile reader: the imperative to students to avoid appearances of anger or bitterness in writing is an attempt to socialize them into the same kinds of ideologies of collegiality that order the relations of their professors, and that are cultural translations of the political dictates of the liberal pluralist state.

In order to reinforce the paradigms of the liberal democratic status quo, liberal pluralism has to be a coercive and intolerant ideology. Pluralists allow "any" approach, as long as it isn't anti-pluralist. Liberal pluralism only permits liberal pluralism, and only as this pluralism is defined and determined by specific relations of domination. In her essay "Context is All: Feminism and Theories of Citizenship," Mary Dietz (1987) illustrates, for instance, how liberal ideals are incompatible with feminism because they guarantee the *individual* "a fair start" in a race where the instructions, vehicles, road, and prizes are unremittingly phallo(go)centric. Dietz demonstrates that the liberal concept of rights, and liberalism's distinction between public and private, cannot speak to the arenas where women have historically been oppressed (marriage, the home, etc.). In liberal society, context is nothing, and individuals are conceived as independent of social and political conditions; thus, the specific forces and values that have shaped women's socializations, identifications, and material existences have no place in constituting the liberal notion of rights.

In the following sections of this chapter, I will develop the implications of the assumptions embedded in the mandate to write for a "general audience." I look at how attempts at "general persuasion" and the construction of audiences as mythical "men on the street" can inhibit student writing and writers, especially in those ubiquitous essay assignments where students are instructed to keep hostile readers in mind and anticipate counterarguments to their own positions.[6] As I hope my discussion of the particular permutations and ramifications of these kinds of constructions of audience will show in section III below, conventional constructions of audience can collude in the reproduction of a liberal pluralism that marginalizes political dissidence and non-normative subjects. I also want to suggest how different conceptualizations of audience may work—for example, the zines I discuss below, which are directed at what Nancy Fraser (1996) has called "subaltern counterpublics," can embody a different relationship to their audience than that envisaged by the common construction of audience in composition classes, and can have formative consequences for writers, readers, and our understandings of politics, rhetoric, and public space.

III. ALTERNATE MODELS

Here, I look briefly at two examples of writing that I think resist contemporary composition's conventional understanding of audience, both in order to show what kinds of productive work these resistant discourses may be said to be doing, and to suggest possibilities for student writing that move beyond commonplaces about audience. First, I'll discuss the phenomenon of zines; then I'll consider some of bell hooks' work.

Stephen Duncombe describes zines as "noncommercial, nonprofessional, small-circulation magazines which their creators produce, publish, and distribute by themselves . . . Zines are an individualist medium, but as a medium their primary function is communication. As such, zines are as much about the communities that arise out of their circulation as they are artifacts of personal expression" (Duncombe 1997, 6, 45). Amy Wan elaborates on the relationship of zines to dominant popular discourse: "Zines are a perfect example of an information source that was not created by a corporate conglomerate (unlike almost all news from mainstream television and newspapers). . . . Their mere existence disrupts the monotone drone of mainstream media; they say something different and their agendas are self-imposed, rather than dictated by advertisers or corporate owners" (Wan 1999, 17). Given the specialized subject matter of many zines, and their appeal to a correspondingly specialized audience, it's hardly surprising that zines often address subjects or perspectives that are ignored or suppressed in corporate media (e.g., note the titles of the zines *We Like Poo* (n.d.) and *Diseased Pariah News* (1990–94) — the latter was an infamous zine created by and for gay men with AIDS in the early 1990s).

The taboo content of many zines is only one of the ways in which zines disrupt prevailing assumptions about composition and the teaching of writing. The tones of campiness, flippancy, sarcasm, outrageousness, anger, and fuck-youness that characterize many zines fly in the face of the rationality, decorum, measured language, and respect for the reader demanded of college composition. Of course, these dispassionate tones of expected expository writing assume that one's reader is potentially hostile, but also a potential convert to one's argument. These imperatives disallow the possibility—and the productive results—of writing for an already sympathetic reader, despite the reality that many professional writers do so. Repudiating decorum is a way of moving beyond the basics of a topic—the necessary foundational explanations for ignorant or hostile audiences—and of grappling with more complex and difficult issues. The repudiation of decorum also provides an opportunity to explore the role that emotion can play in writing, the power that rage can produce, the pleasure of writing loudly and with excess, and the liberation that comes with writing with a blatant disregard for—or even a scathing mockery of—those who disagree with you. These pleasures and powers are too often denied to composition students.

"A student handbook for writing and learning" informs students that "the only kind of thinking that will hold up under careful examination by your audience is logical thinking—thinking that is reasonable, reliable, and above all, believable" (Sebranek, Meyer, and Kemper 1996, 558). But zine writers often reject the normalizing notions that reason equals logic and emotion equals illogic, and reject the assumption that illogic doesn't have value in the first place.[7] In studying and creating zines, students can begin to question this binary; they also begin to ask why certain discursive modes are constructed as more rational than others, and what these constructions indicate about cultural forces and expectations. Obviously, then, writers of zines have a very different conception of their audience when compared with the college writer imagined in most composition handbooks. Since zines are often so specialized, zine writers often have a very specific audience in mind, thus defying the imperative to write to the mythical "man on the street."

Because of the impolitic tone of many zines, the liberal pluralist mandate to write to a general audience—an always potentially persuadable audience—is replaced by writing tailored to a material community. When I have my composition students create zines, I require that students distribute them to their intended audiences and report back on their reactions. Ironically, as I have pointed out in previous chapters, the imperative in composition studies that effective writers have a concrete sense of their audience is seldom translated into pedagogical praxis: fictitious constructs of how a generic audience might react to a student text often conjure up the far-from-generic person of the teacher, violating axiom 4 of *Upsetting Composition Commonplaces* that insists students are "real" writers. Work with zines not only enables students to escape the ideological dictates of liberal pluralism, but also serves an immediate pedagogical function by giving them a much sharper and more immediate sense of their readers. Zines that my and my colleagues' students have created include the feminist *The Church of Perpetual Male Bashing: God Help You!* (1997), which assumes that all women share the composers' conviction that heterosexual men need to be "taken down"; *Rage Against the University!* (2006), which extols the virtues of directing one's rage against university administrators and takes for granted the fact that every reader is already an activist and comrade; *Objectaphilia* (n.d.), which takes "the desire to engage in sexual activities with household objects" seriously and unashamedly; and *BRITE (brown/white) Ideas!* (2005), a zine touting itself as "Canada's first brown people zine." These zines illustrate the productive possibilities that come with writing for specific constituencies.[8]

Turning now to a discussion of bell hooks' work, I want to create a juxtaposition between decidedly different kinds of discourses (hooks 1989, 1990, 1992, 1994a, 1994b, 1994c, 1994d, 2000). While zines (both the phenomenon and the texts) seem to be prima facie resistant on so many levels to the conventionalized academic discourses constructed and taught in composition classes, hooks' work—the early work, in particular—at first glance might appear to be more indebted to conventional tropes of "scholarly" writing. Although hooks writes for a wide audience, and her work is read in- and outside academia, it certainly seems more academic than zines. Moreover, hooks' articles and books are frequently taught in academic settings (including university first-year composition classes), and are often the subject of analysis and argumentation in student writing. Yet, composition students are seldom encouraged to model their writing after hooks', and, in fact, as I discuss below, some of hooks' writing resists many of the commonplaces that inform the teaching of expository writing at US universities. My choice of hooks as exemplar is also purposeful, in order to illustrate my assertion that commonly repeated (and seldom interrogated) composition truisms about audience are far from politically baggage-free.

I have had numerous opportunities to assign hooks' early articles and books to my composition students at different institutions and across all levels of writing classes, and have found, without fail, that the majority of my students (almost always excluding the black students in the class) reacted with defensiveness and hostility to the hooks texts that treat questions around race. These students always framed this response as a critique of hooks' writing style, rather than as a reaction to the (racial) politics or arguments that hooks is advancing. (Anecdotal reports from colleagues confirm that their students respond in the same way.) When my students read one of hooks' articles about the racial politics of Madonna's music videos and other work, many often attacked hooks' assertions and expressed outrage at the way in which hooks uses anecdotal evidence to advance her argument that Madonna's work and her adulation by white audiences in the 1980s and 1990s were symptomatic of a white privilege that depoliticized African-American identity, while continuing to demonize black women's bodies. At one point in the piece, hooks notes Madonna's appropriation of black culture: "Perhaps that is why so many of the grown black women I spoke with about Madonna had no interest in her as a cultural icon and said things like 'The bitch can't even sing'" (hooks 1992, 157). Students often reacted to this anecdote with visible anger, denouncing hooks' evidence as unreliable and unscholarly, and her argument as unpersuasive. When hooks reflects on Madonna's film, *Truth or Dare*, my students' outrage intensified: "Joking about the film with other black folk, we commented that Madonna must have searched long and hard to find a black female that was not a good dancer" (163). They accused hooks of perpetuating racist stereotypes, of making wild generalizations, and of not providing any evidence to support her claims.

My point is not only that by inculcating in students the belief that very limited modes of persuasion are the only acceptable means of expository expression we are drastically narrowing their view of the kinds of texts and discourses that work, that have an effect on the world, and that might give them pleasure and pause, but also that there is a political valence to my students' complaints about hooks. By expecting hooks to lay out arguments that her text takes for granted, students are denying her the opportunity to move past very basic assertions (particularly about race). As I suggested above, zines are able to perform a similar move, by addressing a specialized audience and thus being able to assume that their readers share certain values and assumptions. More perniciously, though, my students' complaints against hooks implicitly demand that she centralize non-black readers, making their concerns her focal ones, and thus possibly remarginalizing black readers (and black experiences). Christian Weisser (2008, 611) explains, "counter publics can also function as sites of safety, encouragement, and nurturing," and, if we conceptualize the audiences addressed in zines and hooks' work as "counterpublics," then we can also see the rhetorical strategies used by the authors of these texts as nurturing such counterpublics by moving them "from margin to center" (to use the subtitle of hooks' book on feminist theory) and establishing their positions as neither defensive nor minor.[9] Conventional composition understandings of "counterargument" merely follow the liberal pluralist mandate to situate a limited range of positions under an umbrella that occludes radical difference. As Stanley Fish states, "The liberal strategy is to devise (or attempt to devise) procedural mechanisms that are neutral with respect to point of view and therefore can serve to frame partisan debates in a nonpartisan manner" (Fish 1994, 16). (More on the question of partiality in the next chapter.)

My students' complaints about hooks' rhetorical strategies also have broader epistemological and politically-charged import, since the dismissal of hooks' anecdotal evidence and personal experience as not sufficiently scholarly or persuasive assumes that "scholarly" rhetorical strategies are universally and unideologically valued, and denies the material reality of racist epistemologies of knowledge and knowledge-production that might erase black subjects from scholarship and deem personal experience "not scholarly"—a point hooks herself makes in *Teaching to Transgress: Education as the Practice of Freedom* (hooks 1994c, 89–90). This skepticism of scholarly objectivity was an axiom of second-wave feminist critiques of the presumptions to universality of a long tradition of androcentric scholarship in many disciplines.[10] Matters of tone and voice also come into play here, as they do in the zines' eschewing of hegemonic expectations of "politeness" and "civility" that are ubiquitous in college composition pedagogy. These, too, are often entrenched in certain class values and political ideologies, and dominant conceptualizations of desirable tone and voice are then used to demonize women and other subaltern subjects.[11] Many of my students are wont to construct hooks as an "angry black woman" (usually without using these words, of course), inevitably oblivious of how much more generously they might read a white male author's text written in a similar tone and style. (Their constructions of hooks as an "angry black woman" no doubt also influence their failure to see any humor in the above two quotes from hooks' Madonna article).[12]

Both the zines and hooks' texts pay less attention to trying to convince imagined adversaries than is usually demanded of "persuasive" writing in composition classrooms. I should reiterate that I do not mean to suggest that counterarguments or consideration of hostile audiences are always politically compromised endeavors. Certainly there is a valuable place for such strategies/dispositions in a variety of texts and contexts. However, I am concerned about the monolithic force these imperatives have accumulated in composition pedagogy, resulting in many other politically and aesthetically valuable types of writing being demonized and even prohibited. The fetishization of "counterarguments," and the need to "counter" them, not only centralizes and normalizes hegemonic ideologies—as I have suggested above—but is also caught up in larger nods to "objectivity" (the subject of the following chapter), since the addressing of counterarguments is supposed to show one's God-like mastery of the topic at hand. The refusal of these injunctions produces discourse that potentially resists such aspirations to mastery, and that has different effects and functions—indeed, situating language, ideas, and writers differently in relation to readers and the world at large.

One possible critique of my suspicion of audience commonplaces might feel that a retreat from the conventions of civility and counterargument invites the loss of political and intellectual rigor, that such a retreat is accompanied by anti-intellectualism—the kind of uncritical expressivism exposed so pointedly by Bartholomae (1995) and others—or anything goes pluralism. If we are not going to insist on careful argumentation, the objection might say, "Aren't we inviting in the worst kind of impressionism? Might we be substituting emotion for careful reflection? Don't we run the risk of being forced to validate sloppy or even untenable arguments?" However, I am not arguing against evaluation or judgment, whether moral, political, aesthetic, or pedagogical. Something is not immune from critique merely because it imagines and enacts a different kind of relationship to its audience. We do, will continue to, and should make these kinds of evaluations and judgments, whether of arguments, anecdotes, narratives, outbursts, or any other discourse. Of course, we need to recognize that these judgments are never objective, and can never be objective (more on this in the next chapter). Also, this recognition must apply as much to an evaluation of an argument essay as to an evaluation of a poem or a picture. What changes then, is not a movement from evaluation to lack of evaluation, but rather a shift in the evaluation criteria that accompanies the opening up of forms that are assigned and produced in the writing classroom.

IV. PRESSING BOUNDARIES

Moving alongside, out from, and beyond narrow expectations around audience in the composition classroom can prove productive for students in terms of both reading and writing. If students aren't only looking for (and aren't trained to only look for) narrowly and singularly conceived notions of audience in their nonfiction reading, they may be open to being moved and challenged and inspired by different rhetorics (and other kinds of argument)—in addition to being critical of these texts, of course.[13] They already do this in their reading of other kinds of texts (e.g., novels), but the inability to apply reading strategies across genres is one lamentable symptom of the disjunction we in composition have promulgated between the reading of fiction and expository texts that I set out in axiom 3 (Writing Is Writing) and discussed in detail in chapter 3. By seeing how a variety of writing strategies work, or do not work, the possibilities of writing (including academic writing) are also expanded and multiplied for students.

Here are some possibilities for student writing (these are seed ideas for further development/exploration, rather than fully fleshed-out assignment prompts):

- Create a zine.
- Write a manifesto.

Manifestos can deploy similar rhetorical strategies to zines. Manifestos are typically "one-sided," and therefore usually aren't beholden to the "consider counterarguments" imperative. In addition, they often use strident or angry tones, thus resisting the politeness imperatives that are commonly embedded in narrow constructions of argument and college composition (and academic writing) in general. It helps to provide a variety of sample manifestos for students to study beforehand, and not just manifestos from mainstream political parties (which tend to be geared toward offending as few people as possible), but also more radical or enigmatic texts like Valerie Solanas' (1991) *The Scum Manifesto* or Francis Picabia's (2000) "DADA Manifesto." A manifesto assignment can allow students to experience the pleasures and gains (and drawbacks) of writing uncensored ideas in "extreme language," without the sometimes paralyzing preoccupation with naysayers and conventions of hegemonic academic style and tone.

- After reading Michelle Cliff's "If I Could Write This in Fire, I Would Write This in Fire," write something in fire.

The "fire" here refers to Cliff's political and personal anger and fierceness, and how words can be used to convey "fire" (Cliff 2008). Like the zine and manifesto assignments, this one encourages students to write with passion, contravening the dispassionate tones they are usually encouraged to adopt in their academic essays (students have often internalized this encouragement quite effectively).

The merits and losses of displacing or repressing passion and emotion in certain types of writing can be a rich topic of discussion before, during, and after students work on this assignment. We often feel rage about certain topics, and sometimes rage is not only justified but is even called for. These kinds of discussions can lead to important interrogations of academic, ideological, class-based, racialized, and gendered notions of "appropriateness" and "control." They help us to complicate clichés about audience and unpack the notion of the "general audience" that Rooney (1989) sees as a construct of liberal pluralism. As Weisser argues, "Counterpublics . . . often welcome or encourage anger and other emotions as tools of engagement. Rather than seeing anger as a violation of good will, counterpublics may be more open to seeing it as a *demonstration* of good will" (Weisser 2008, 613).

- Using bell hooks' concept of cultural criticism ("to take another look, to contest, to interrogate, and in some cases to recover and redeem" [hooks 1994b, 5]) and hooks' own prose as a model, analyze a popular culture text in a way that resists conventional understandings.

As with the previous suggestions, this assignment liberates students from the need to use cool language and cautious ideas, but here these liberations specifically come in the service of critical takes on popular culture and conventional readings of particular popular culture texts. Via hooks' prose style and her project of reading against the grain, students contest hegemonic ideologies around race, class, and gender. hooks argues that this kind of work teaches critical thinking and promotes a liberatory pedagogy (hooks 1994b, 5), and it seems especially appropriate for courses and institutions with social justice commitments.

- Write a research paper for an audience that already shares some or all of your assumptions about your topic.

The last assignment might be especially useful in preparing students for higher-level academic writing, where scholars situate their work in dialogue with other members of relatively small interpretive communities. The assignment does create a problem: how can students and teachers who do not have the specialized disciplinary knowledge that the topics assume appropriately respond to and evaluate student work? This question might fruitfully invite interrogations of the composition class' appropriateness as an audience of student writing, the role of teachers and fellow students in reading and responding to student writing, and evaluation and grading. However, in keeping with one of the motifs of this book, and in solidarity with the many composition scholars, teachers, and writers who have lamented composition's service imperative, I also want to insist on the value of writing assignments and activities that—although taking place in the university—are not purely geared toward the university, as well as the value of making spaces for such "non-university writing" in composition classes. These projects—in addition to expanding understandings of university reading and writing, especially expository reading and writing in the composition classroom—can help students understand how a broader range of writing and thinking works, and understand and engage with the value of a broader range of writing.

NOTES

1. For discussion of the imperative in composition scholarship and pedagogy that students write to a "real" audience, see Isaacs and Jackson (2001) and Lu (1994). For a discussion of this imperative in high schools, see "Writing Improves When Publishing is the Goal" (2006). For a rejoinder to composition's fashionable insistence on audience awareness, see Peter Elbow's (1987) meditation on the pleasures of not writing for an audience, as well as on how constructing an audience in the early stages of the writing process can be paralyzing for (student) writers.

2. Rebecca Moore Howard (2012) coined the term "quote mining."

3. Important critiques have been offered of the standardized essay form, arguing that form constrains meaning, and that form determines what and who essays—academic essays, in particular—privilege, and what, by definition, they must exclude from their purview (e.g., Annas 2003; Fort 1975; Weathers 1980). While I do believe that form determines content to the extent that some ideas may be inexpressible in particular forms—forms serve as terministic screens—I think a too simplistic characterization of any form assumes that it cannot be manipulated for

diverse ends, and that formal constraints can't themselves enable innovative recombinations that explode meaning. Sometimes being forced to
push language within and against the boundaries of a particular form
forces new and unanticipated configurations, allowing for unexpected
meanings that may not be possible when one can determine in advance
that a particular form will convey a particular meaning.

The idea of constraints in poetry or music come to mind here, and
the work of the Oulipo writers, or Adorno's analysis of twelve-tone music.
Formal limitation can unleash a torrent of combinations within a text, so
much that meaning ultimately strains against form. Fixed form can force
one to use it very purposefully. Paradoxically, it can also propel unanticipated and new meaning when content strains against it, such as when
composers are inspired or forced to manipulate texts in innovative ways
in order to conform to form, in order to make desirable meaning within
prescribed forms. In any case, as Foucault and other poststructuralists
would say, it's a delusion to imagine that one can stand outside power
(form)—freedom is itself a construction of power. When form is not up
for grabs, then the myth of its freedom cannot be entertained, either. Or,
as David Bartholomae (1995) translated this recognition into composition studies, the metacognition of the academic essay gives the lie to the
truth of personal narrative.

For further efforts to recover, expand, and reconceptualize the essay
form, see Covino (1988a; 1988b), Winterowd (1994). The relationship
of classical rhetoric to some of these composition commonplaces is contested. Whereas some scholars blame "Aristotelian rhetoric" for many of
the ills embodied in contemporary composition pedagogy (e.g., Hawk
2007; Jolliffe 1996), others like Covino (1988b), Spellmeyer (1993), and
Zeiger (1985) attempt to rehabilitate classical rhetoric by claiming it has
been misread or ignored in contemporary composition. Without weigh-
ing in on the persuasiveness of these claims, I want to note that attempts
to rehabilitate Aristotle and co. are in and of themselves problematic
insofar as they reproduce a Western rhetorical canon, especially in the
face of contemporary postcolonial and other critiques of this canon, as
well as critiques of the construction of rhetorical history as originating in
the classical West (e.g., Baca 2008; Powell 2012).

4.   For discussion and critique of agonism in composition, see Gearhart
(2003), Jolliffe (1996), and Vidali (2011). For a critique of the
"technology of assertion" in composition, see Olson (1999). Susan
Jarratt (2003) expresses skepticism of the "resistance to conflict" that
marks the confluence of feminism and composition, arguing that the
eschewal of conflict can serve to reinforce existing power relations by
refusing to interrogate the inequities that inform these relations. For
Jarratt, a resistance to conflict has the effect of an acquiescence, which
tacitly endorses the status quo, since confrontation (and conflict) are
required to expose, denaturalize, and ultimately upset those norms and
hegemonies.

5.   For some critiques of argument and the teaching of argument, see Bay
(2002), Cohen (2011), Haynes (2003), and Vitanza (1991).

6. See Barnard (2005) for further elaboration of this conjunction between liberal pluralism and specific constructions of argument.

7. For an overview of recent rhetoric on emotion, and a nuanced argument for the importance of considering emotion when crafting rhetorical appeals, see Jackson (2011). See Worsham (2002) for a critique of the demonization of anger/shame/bitterness. For some relevant critiques of reason/rationality, see Bernard-Donals (2008) and Wiederhold (2008).

8. The above paragraphs on zines are excerpted from a collaborative article written by Aneil Rallin and me, published in *Reflections: A Journal of Public Rhetoric, Civic Writing, and Service Learning* (Rallin and Barnard 2008). I thank Aneil for his enthusiastic permission to use that material here. For further discussion of zines, see Barnard (1996).

9. For a more detailed discussion of some of these issues in the context of separatism, see Barnard (1998).

10. For further discussion of personal experience as evidence in academic writing, see Spigelman (2004).

11. See Barnard (2005) for further discussion of the coercions that can masquerade as civility.

12. For further discussion of the politics of style, and the ways in which students can be socialized into becoming the guardians of hegemonic academic standards, see Barnard (2009).

13. See Barnard (2009) for a case study of students enforcing rigid rules of argument in their reading of published texts.

7
OBJECTIVITY

In 1988, William Covino succinctly articulated the challenges poststructuralism posed to humanist composition practices and theory: "The epistemological crisis of this century—the failure of objectivity, Cartesian rationality, and detachment to account for our complicated perception of a world in flux where matters are never settled—has called into question writing that tries to maintain unity, coherence, perspicuity, and certainty, writing that Edward Said has called 'preservative' rather than 'investigative'" (Covino 1988a, 121). This chapter is especially concerned with the first concept on Covino's list, objectivity, though perceptions and constructions of rationality and detachment are inextricably linked with assumptions about and imperatives for objectivity. My goal here is to unpack the explicit and tacit appeals to objectivity that inform composition—particularly the discourses around grading, assessment, and the dominant ways of teaching expository essays and research in first-year composition classes—and suggest how these appeals shape and undo composition's self-understanding and future potential.

I. MYTHS OF OBJECTIVITY

Much like other liberal commonplaces such as clarity, civility, and multiculturalism, objectivity presents itself as commonsensical and transparent as it masks ideological affiliations.[1] This is precisely why its hold is so powerful. Liberal pluralism allows for any point of view as long as it isn't at odds with liberal pluralism![2] Thus, liberal pluralism constructs itself as the model of tolerance (all points of view are welcome) while in effect shoring up its own power. Objectivity is deployed to a parallel ingenuous effect.

DOI: 10.7330/9780874219470.c007

As I suggested in chapter 5, critiques of objectivity over the past half century have been wide-ranging. Feminist, anti-racist, LGBT/queer, Marxist, disability, and other scholars and activists have demonstrated that that which was passed off as universal was, in fact, quite particular (in most cases representing the interests and values of dominant groups). Critical legal studies gave the lie to the law's objectivity, while critical race studies deconstructed the supposedly scientific bases of racial categorizations. Pretensions to objectivity were assailed in the sciences, as well as in social science disciplines like history and anthropology.[3] Postcolonial studies also gave the lie to universalism, fuelled by anti-colonial resistance to ethnocentric generalizations propelled from and by the West in the service of the colonial project and the projection of the Western subject as "universal man," and aided by poststructuralism's radical suspicion of humanist epistemologies of self and subjectivity. Trinh T. Minh-ha notes of the "*anonymous* all-male, and predominantly white collective entity named *he*" (Trinh 1989, 48–49, emphasis original) whom she wishes to "undo": "I am temporarily referring to him in the third person, the pronoun of the non-person, since he claims to be the spokesman for the entire human race—never hesitating to speak about and for a vague entity named *man* whose putative universality no longer fools anyone." Ideologies of universality and objectivity are complementary bulwarks in humanist epistemologies, which envisage truth and essential humanness as waiting to be discovered beneath layers of ideology, distorting rhetoric, and superficial difference. Using renowned ethnographer Bronislaw Malinowski (whom she doesn't refer to by name, deploying instead the scathing moniker "the Great Master") as a case study, Trinh goes on to adumbrate the ways in which anthropologists impose their own values onto their subjects and are invariably able to find "evidence" to support their biases, all the while forwarding their agendas in the name of truth and objectivity, since this is what they yearn for. While anthropologists present their informants' testimony as "gossip," they don't see their own discourse as "gossip" (i.e., local, personal, idiosyncratic)—it is constructed as scientific, truthful, objective, and universal (69–71). "Can one 'look for a structure' without structuring?" Trinh asks rhetorically (141).

In exposing traditional ethnography's masculinist, imperialist, and racist biases, Trinh pays special attention to the writing practices embedded in this ethnographic work, thus suggesting a crucial connection between her disciplinary resistance and composition:

> Are we dealing here with the old rule of objectivity we have been taught in school in every composition class? Achieve distance, they keep on saying, as much distance from your own voice as possible. Don't direct the reader's attention to yourself, don't fiddle with words just to show off. For a woman, such a distance easily takes on the face of Alienation. She must *learn* not only to impersonalize the voice she stole or borrowed, but also to internalize gradually the impersonal generic interpretation of masculine pronouns and nouns. (Trinh 1989, 27)

In literary studies, the myth of the objectivity of the literary canon was exploded as canons were expanded, counter-canons were established, and the idea of canonicity itself was questioned beginning in the 1960s. And with the rise of critical pedagogy's interrogation of classroom texts and methodologies, one could no longer claim that teaching was or could be objective.

As usual, composition is a bit behind the theory curve, but growing suspicion around standardized tests, rubrics, and assessment practices in composition (e.g., Inoue and Poe 2012; Wilson 2008) has recently tempered competing efforts to make the field respectably scientific (more on this later). The current move at many US universities to student-directed self-placement in college composition courses, rather than the previous practice of relying on scores from standardized tests to place students in composition classes, is indicative of the success of this suspicion. Other work in composition that is critical of composition's faith in objectivity comes from feminist, poststructuralist, and anti-imperialist composition theorists. For instance, Gary Olson critiqued the dominance of "the rhetoric of assertion," via an analysis of the ruse of objectivity presented by science and "its unquestioned compulsion to assert truth" (Olson 1999, 10). And, in her Chair's address at the 2012 Conference on College Composition and Communication (CCCC) convention, Malea Powell explicitly evoked personal stories and storytelling as anti-imperialist interventions into the Western rhetorical tradition, as well as into composition's privileging of the impersonal essay form.[4]

In all of these cases, it was not just the content or conclusion of a particular field or knowledge base that was questioned, but methodology itself was also the object of critique. Certain methodologies of research, teaching, writing, and reading could be coded as masculinist. Others could be coded as feminist. Some might be multiple, inconsistent, or something else altogether. Nevertheless, each decision implies certain values and excludes others. There is no neutrality—as this multifaceted and enormous body of new work taught us along with poststructuralist philosophers like Foucault, it's not possible to stand outside oneself, in a position of no location, as a subject who is a clean slate. One cannot *not* have values. And while one may be able to suppress certain values in certain circumstances, every act of reading, writing, teaching, thinking, and testing is value-laden nonetheless. Objectivity is a delusion. Even multiple choice tests can no longer get away with claiming to be objective, thanks to critiques of the race and class biases undergirding standardized tests like the SAT that have gained national attention over the past two decades (see, for example, Jencks and Phillips 1998). This work has also informed and followed from the 1974 CCCC resolution on Students' Right to Their Own Language, and from a plethora of compositionists and reading scholars showing (1) how class and race formations impact students' likelihood of passing university gatekeepers, (2) the biases that inform hegemonic standards of language competence and grammatical correctness (e.g., Young 2009), and (3) the ways in which our ideas of "error" are socially constructed (e.g., Horner 1992; Williams 1981).

Many social justice advocates have insisted that objectivity not even be sought in the first place. To remain "neutral" in cases of injustice is to condone the status quo, and to refuse to speak out against inequity and oppression is to abdicate one's moral and ethical responsibility as a scholar, teacher, and member of society. Reflecting on Freire's influence on her and on her own education in segregated black schools in the South, bell hooks articulates her own political commitment as a teacher: "I understood from the teachers in those segregated schools that the work of any teacher committed to the full self-realization of students was necessarily and fundamentally radical, that ideas were not neutral, that to teach in a way that liberates, that expands consciousness, that awakens, is to challenge domination at its very core" (hooks 2000, 80). These arguments beg the question of how one decides what justice is, a point to which I will return below.

II. THE RESILIENCE OF OBJECTIVITY

Despite these critiques, objectivity—or at least its lure— remains resilient. This is equally true in lay culture as it is in academia. In the latter, journalism students continue to be schooled in the imperatives of objectivity (see, for example, Greenwald 2012), law schools still take the desirability of judicial objectivity as axiomatic, and future teachers are taught supposedly objective grading practices, despite—and sometimes as a reaction against—the ascendance of poststructuralist theory in multiple academic disciplines. In many cases, the lessons of poststructuralism, feminism, and other critiques of the putatively universal have been co-opted and deradicalized. Thus the attacks on the literary canon are sometimes met merely with attempts to expand the canon, keeping the concept of canonicity intact, and the assumption that one can objectively determine which texts are greater or more universal than others unquestioned.[5]

Liberals and the anti-postmodern Left are just as guilty as everyone else in this fetishization (or, at least, lipservice to this effect) of facts and objectivity. In political culture, some Leftists— often including scholars and activists who have participated in the critiques of universality chronicled above (e.g., Edward Said 1979, Noam Chomsky 1987)—fearful of relativism and hostile to postmodernism's perceived apoliticism, cling to objectivity. Unwilling to give up facts and truth, they ultimately reinscribe the humanism that constructed "universal man" in the first place.[6] As if facts will save us. In the popular media run up to the 2012 US presidential election, Al Sharpton (2012) insisted on MSNBC on the "facts" of Barack Obama's presidency, in response to Republican criticisms of Obama as "the most divisive president ever." "Reality" is matter-of-factly materialized and reduced to occlude the inevitability of it as mediated and interpreted, and, in many instances, to deny the possibility of any position outside narrowly conceived political binarisms (Republicans vs. Democrats), constructed in the service of corporate capitalism. While this deference to "facts" might be rationalized as strategic and politically expedient for Said, Chomsky, and Sharpton, it in effect sets the stage for the infinitely cyclical relativism of competing narratives that marshal "facts" at the expense of insisting on ethical and social appeals—"facts" become the escape from having to make an argument about the value of a particular policy, practice, or belief.

In US academia—and in highly charged conflicts around pedagogy and curricula, in particular—and radiating out into mass media, the ruse of "objectivity" came into particularly sharp focus with the culture wars of the 1990s, including attacks by conservatives on affirmative action programs and multiculturalism. In composition, this fracas was sharply played out around Linda Brodkey's "Writing About Difference" course at The University of Texas, where the course's opponents attacked it for being biased and demanded that the course focus on "composition" rather than "politics," apparently oblivious of the politics in their own constructions of "composition" (Brodkey 1996, especially 181ff.). Twenty plus years later, some residual resistance to cultural studies and social constructionist theories and methods of teaching composition occasionally reappear (e.g., Fulkerson 2005), but by and large socially committed composition has won the day.

However, objectivity has not yet been laid to rest. The spaces in composition where appeals to, constructions of, and assumptions of objectivity continue to hold sway are many and varied, and often enable and inform—or are informed and enabled by—social and political deployments of discourses about and around objectivity in the public sphere. For instance, as I noted in chapter 1, composition students' ideas about the possibility and desirability (and even necessity) of objectivity may reflect uncritical commonplaces about objectivity that circulate in the legal and journalistic realms, and—as I've suggested above—that are even taught (and enforced) by their college teachers in various disciplines. In turn, the academic training of law students, journalists, and composition students may lead to a recapitulation of the obeisance to objectivity once these students graduate and become the new demarcators and gatekeepers of their professions. These bidirectional and mutually reinforcing objectivity imperatives may significantly impact both academic and extra-academic realms. Maja Wilson points out, for example, that the United States' infamous, much discredited (and now significantly retreated from) No Child Left Behind Act of 2001 (NCLB) called for the "achievement gap" among differently performing school students to be closed using "effective, scientifically based instructional strategies" (Wilson 2008, xxii). The cluster of connotations assumed and hidden beneath the phrase "scientifically based" can be credibly seen as the enforcer of a regime of standardized testing that became the uncritical backbone of NCLB, the bane of high school teachers throughout the country, and the object of much scholarship and commentary from experts in composition and education, who argued its pedagogical, theoretical, and political unsoundness.[7] In this case, a science-based regimen, with its attendant respect earned through facts, data, and objectivity, is seen as the antidote to the partial and impressionistic (humanities-based) assessments of the professional instructors who are actually teaching the children in question, as the idea of scientific objectivity shuttles uncritically between political and academic institutions.

III. ASSESSMENT IN COMPOSITION

Perhaps composition's version of the "scientifically based instructional strategies" might be the ubiquitous timed essay assignments that still serve as writing assessment tools on many college campuses in the United States and elsewhere. I am not speaking here of the in-class essay exams that faculty across the disciplines might assign in their classes in order to assess students' content knowledge, though sometimes composition faculty—despite their loyalty to process theory—also assign in-class timed essays, often with the justification that these will better prepare students to write essay exams in other disciplines, will help ensure that composition students' other work is truly their own, or will give students "practice" in writing the kinds of essays that various entrance and exit placement and assessment protocols will require. Instead, I have in mind the program- and university-wide assessment protocols, often run by, graded by, and prepared for by composition faculty and administrators. At many universities, for example, all students are required to demonstrate "writing proficiency" beyond first-year composition before they graduate, and must do so by receiving a passing score on a timed essay test, independent of any courses they may be taking. The scoring procedure is familiar to compositionists, who have participated in so many mass writing exams: students' names may not appear on their essays; graders are "normed" using sample student papers; they score "live" papers anonymously and without seeing other graders' scores; each paper is read and scored by two graders; papers with split scores are read by a third reader; and so on.

Almost every component of this protocol is putatively about objectivity—ensuring it, promoting it, believing in it, protecting it. It is assumed, for instance, that grading is more objective when papers are graded by strangers rather than the student's instructor. Or if you don't know a student's name, you won't be (unconsciously) influenced to make assumptions about the student's English language competency, based on the ethnic or national identifications the name may evoke. Or if you spend enough time "training" readers with rubrics and sample papers, they will score similarly and more in line with the demands of the rubric, rather than based on their own personal writing preferences and grading biases. But these tactics are ruses, of course. Yes, readers may be socialized to score papers a certain way, but that "certain way" itself enacts particular biases, privileging some components of student writing over others, etc. And, given the scholarship that has demonstrated that English Language Learners are disproportionately disadvantaged when students are required to compose timed essays instead of untimed essays,[8] the very form of the assessment cannot be considered objective in the first place.

My point here is not that untimed essays should replace timed essays as a method of assessment that will create less biases (though I certainly advocate such a change), but rather to draw attention to some of the ways in which outdated and discredited inferences about objectivity are inextricably intricated in common composition practices, and to underscore my reminder that no form of assessment can be objective. Similar objectivity assumptions often inform other composition assessment practices, such as group portfolio scorings.

IV. COMPOSITION PEDAGOGY

Objectivity also makes its way into composition pedagogy in argument essays, research papers, work with sources, and general attitudes about the essay as a genre. At institutions where I have taught, for instance, students in our first-year writing courses were instructed early on in the semester how to summarize texts they read, with summary being clearly distinguished from "interpretation," as if it were possible to objectively condense and rephrase what another writer said without mediating the original text in any way. (The fact that many of these teachers had expertise in literary studies and knew well the admonition against the "heresy of paraphrase" when it comes to reading poetry further highlights the destructive effects of the distinction between creative and expository writing that composition has advanced in recent years, and that I have been critiquing in axiom 3 and throughout this book.) This is supposed to prepare students for engaging effectively with secondary sources, and to preempt the common problem of student writers making assertions about sources they have "misread" or not understood. I certainly understand that there are problems of students not reading sources carefully, closely, or fully, or not understanding what they are reading (either holistically or at the sentence level). These difficulties are to be expected, given the challenges of the sources that students are often expected to grapple with. However, to suggest that there is a "correct" reading of a source or a "correct summary" of a source—and that reading and summary don't involve processes of selection, disposition, and viewpoint that are, by definition, interested—is not only to promote intellectually, pedagogically, and politically dishonest and untenable epistemologies, but also to compound the difficulty for students by creating reading anxiety and writing paralysis associated with the need to find and articulate the one "correct" answer that these simplistic distinctions between summary and analysis imply.

Poststructuralism's attention to the embeddedness of mediation and the projections of representation situates *every* representation as an interpretation. When representation is coded within the (1) limitations, (2) highly conventionalized arbitrariness, and (3) meaning-making formativity of language, it makes no sense to think of any representation as unmediated. While I concede that it is possible to "misread" a text in the sense that one cannot credibly support one's reading with evidence from the text, I want to caution against many of the problematic assumptions that underlie the injunction to summarize, as well as constructions of summary, not least the imputation that an "accurate" summary will correctly convey authorial intent, a composition trap I interrogated at length in chapter 3.

Prescriptive and simplistic accounts of summary punctuate composition textbooks, pedagogy, and teaching philosophy, and frequently form the foundation of work that students are expected to undertake in their essays and research papers, especially when engaging with primary and secondary sources. In the Expository Reading and Writing Course that high school students in California are now being encouraged to take, written student summaries are an important part of the process of responding to class readings. But the problematic assumptions underlying the understanding of these summaries is made clear in the yes/no questions that students are invited to use when responding to their peers' summaries. One response template asks, "Does the writer keep his/her own opinions *out* of the summary?" followed by the suggestion, "Remember to save your opinion for your response!"—these are supposed to help respondents formulate an explanation to accompany their yes/no answers (California State University Task Force on Expository Reading and Writing 2005, 8, underscore original). The possibility and desirability of "keeping one's opinion out of a summary" is taken for granted, as is the binary opposition between summary and response.

Contemporary composition textbooks continue to obliviously/uncritically promote discredited notions about the possibility and desirability of objectivity. Even the 2012 edition of the compact *Little Penguin Handbook* that I sometimes use in my first-year composition classes—authored by Lester Faigley himself, the father of postmodern composition theory—makes a neat and unproblematized distinction between "summarize" and "analyze" in its tips on how composition students might become critical readers (Faigley 2012, 4–5). Needless to say, "analyze" must always follow "summarize": "On your second reading, analyze the structure using the following questions . . ." (5). The chronology recapitulates the conventional representation of summary as a precursor to analysis, as if one could be done without the other. The composition textbook *Reflections: Patterns for Reading and Writing* similarly instructs students: "Your summary should be a factual, brief reporting of the key idea. Do not include your own impressions, reactions or responses" (McWhorter 2013, 39). While so much college work seems to be dedicated to showing how "facts lie," and how "facts" can be manipulated, first-year composition textbooks like these blithely construct an anachronistic epistemology of scientific truth and unassailable facts. As the third edition of *The McGraw-Hill Guide: Writing for College, Writing for Life* so infelicitously puts it in a chapter on evaluative writing, "Because numerical information is verifiable and is not a matter of opinion, it can be persuasive evidence for your overall evaluation" (Roen, Glau, and Maid 2013, 289).

Objectivity also slips into other facets of essay assignments, often in instructions to students that, although their essays should present a position, this position should be articulated after careful presentation of "both sides" of a particular argument—a covert nod to the ideologies of objectivity that compounds the problems with the counterargument commonplace I discussed in chapter 6. Work with and evaluation of outside sources is made to conform to the same kinds of (false) criteria about objectivity. And again, even new composition textbooks validate these kinds of pedagogies and research/composition dispositions and practices. The second edition of Rebecca Moore Howard's (2014) *Writing Matters: A Handbook of Writing and Research* urges students to decide if a "source seems objective" in the course of evaluating the reliability of research. However, the tantalizing "seems" in Howard's bulleted header becomes plain old "is" in the explanation that follows: "Does the source have an objective tone . . . Or does it contain emotionally loaded language?" (233). Alas, students are not invited to reflect on how "objectivity" gets constructed, the kinds of values and assumptions that are promoted in the name of objectivity, and—per my discussion of persuasion in the previous chapter—how certain kinds of tones (by students and by the sources these students reference) are demonized in composition while others are privileged, why certain tones are considered objective while others are not, and what particular stakes, interests, and biases inform these kinds of hierarchies. I am not talking here about obscure textbooks or unknown authors. What is particularly distressing about these textbooks is that they are often the work of major and well-regarded scholars in the field of rhetoric and composition, and published by the powerhouse textbook publishers in the field.

In writing center work and other efforts to encourage students to assess their own writing, objectivity is also promoted. Students are supposed to develop an "objective" disposition toward their own writing in order to create the necessary distance that supposedly facilitates effective reflection, assessment, and revision of one's own writing. *Writing Matters* lists seven ways for students to "gain objectivity" about their work, including allowing time between drafts (Howard 2014, 83). As one writing center consultant puts it, "A truly successful moment for me occurs when these students achieve even fleeting objectivity in considering their texts. This moment, however brief, embodies the first step the student takes toward becoming a stronger writer" (Pond 2007, 7). What this "objectivity" usually means is that the student should be ventriloquizing the voices and positions of other potential readers, invariably hostile or indifferent to the argument at hand, as a means of better anticipating and addressing readers' concerns. So much is obscured in this, and (related) matter-of-fact resorts to objectivity (in addition to the theoretical impossibility of objectivity and the political problems around centralizing putatively hostile readers that I discussed in the previous chapter). First, as Trinh (1989), Said (1979), and others have demonstrated in their accounts of the authorial projections that animate scholarly and other scientific endeavors, the writer in this case is necessarily going to impose her own vision of hostile or indifferent readers into her revision agenda, an imposition that is no more objective than the writer's original argument was. Second, the correlated injunction to students that research or expository essays should not include their "opinion" (as attested to by students' frequent misunderstanding of instructions against using the first person in their writing as indicating that their essays should be opinionless) perpetuates the dangerous myth—not unlike the uncritical definition of objective summary—that writing can somehow be neutral, as if a thesis, the decision to include certain kinds of evidence, or even particular word choices don't constitute and convey opinions. I consider this myth, in particular, to be dangerous because it allows students to believe that other kinds of discourse are also objective or neutral, discouraging the critical analysis of all discourse that we should be teaching and students should be learning. Third, the focus on objectivity can lead to the kind of generic prose that students believe demonstrates their objectivity, but that they and their readers may find dull and lifeless.

V. THE STAKES: JUSTIFYING COMPOSITION

One can trace a particular alignment between the ideology of objectivity and the types of argument-focused writing and assignments that, as I mentioned in chapter 3, have become increasingly privileged in composition classes over the past three decades (though, as I noted in chapter 4, a backlash is now under way, with attention returning to narrative and creative writing). Essay assignments that demand "objective" research on the part of students and promote dispassion and distance (a problem I also address in the previous chapter) can be seen to complement "objective" grading practices on the part of instructors, complete with rubrics—succinctly character-ized by Maja Wilson as "the latest sacred cow of writing assess-ment" (Wilson 2008, 2)—and other paraphernalia designed to obfuscate the inevitable (and necessary) subjectivity of grading.

However, the resilience of assumptions and discourses around objectivity in composition theory, pedagogy, and administration can also be attributed to a recurring motif in this book: compo-sition's reactive and defensive need to justify and legitimate its status as a scholarly field, and, in particular, its efforts to per-form this legitimation by marking itself as "scientific," a point I discussed in chapter 2 in relation to the fetishization of clarity in composition. In her 1982 article, "Cognition, Convention, and Certainty: What We Need to Know About Writing," as well as her "Afterthought" to the article published twenty-seven years later in *The Norton Book of Composition Studies*, Patricia Bizzell critiques the uncritical acceptance of scientific claims to objectivity and composition's efforts to produce "objective" scientific research (Bizzell 2009, 494ff.). She sees in these efforts the pursuit of a flawed and harmful (to students) conception of "authoritative certainty." Bizzell writes that "inner-directed" composition theorists "seek a kind of certainty they believe is accessible only to science, and their talk of paradigm-shifting invokes Kuhn to announce that our discipline will soon have a scientific basis." More generally, as Bizzell put it, certainty appeals to compositionists because "until recently composition studies was a low-status enclave it was hard to escape; a powerful theory would help us retaliate against the literary critics who dominate English studies. Moreover, such a theory might help us survive what appears to be the long slide of all humanistic disciplines into a low-status enclave. A scientific-sounding theory promises an 'accountability' hedge against hard times."[9]

In addition, this disciplinary insecurity could be said to create justificatory counter-measures, not just to gain peer and public approval but also to convince and reassure students of composition's value and honor, especially around assessment. If the large body of students who are required (often unwillingly) to complete first-year composition courses, in particular—as well as other types of writing assessment—can be socialized into believing that their work is evaluated objectively (e.g., the assurances that final portfolios will receive "blind" readings by disinterested third parties), then composition can presumably continue its work unquestioned, and students and other university stakeholders can be convinced of its efficacy and value. Tellingly, literary studies feels no need to create campaigns to misleadingly assure students that papers in literature classes are graded objectively—no doubt this difference reflects composition's more tenuous hold on public and academic credibility, though literary studies is hardly a bastion of institutional and cultural respect in the context of rabid anti-intellectualism and the increasing marginalization of the humanities in twenty-first century US. Composition has, in a way, backed itself into a corner by choosing to align itself with science rather than art.

I hint at one of the dangers of this complementarity in the word "unquestioned" in the preceding paragraph. Bizzell elaborates on the consequences of science-based closure, cautioning that the strongest appeal of certainty lies in its promise that composition teachers can socialize students into academic discourse "without having to consider the ethical and political dimensions of this act" (Bizzell 2009, 495). This lure could apply equally to the kinds of writing students do (and the ways in which this writing is constructed) as to the representations of composition grading and assessment: by sidestepping matters of value and failing to question the ideology of objectivity (both in science and in composition), composition pedagogy foregoes the critical thinking opportunities propelled by uncertainty and the larger political interrogation of academic and other institutional discourses, which marginalize composition in the first place and enable and sanction the very social and cultural violences that the critique of objectivity discussed in section I above was designed to expose. I turn to an elaboration of these costs in the following section.

VI. THE COSTS

The costs of composition's clinging to and calcification of objectivity are steep. The disjunctions between our theoretical understandings and our pedagogical and administrative manifestos and practices grow ever more unethical and unsustainable. Our own assessment work becomes difficult to untangle from the exponentially increasing quantity and stakes of standardized testing plaguing education across the board. And student writing that is taught and produced under the regime of objectivity continues to alienate its composers (see Trinh in section I above) and disappoint its readers. I'll briefly discuss a few of the theoretical lacunae implicated in composition's pursuit of objectivity, and then provide some quick elaborations of the pedagogical and writing consequences for composition students.

The common complaint against postmodernism's skittishness around concepts like facts, truth, and objectivity invokes charges of apoliticism and radical relativism that results in an evacuation of ethical and moral judgment of any kind. Lester

Faigley, however, via Lyotard's discussion of Auschwitz, makes exactly the opposite case, showing how dangerous the uncritical belief in and reliance on foundationalism can be: when facts become the only acceptable bottom line, then the absence of facts (or the inability to prove them) invalidates one's argument, no matter how moral or "true" it might be (Faigley 1992, 234). This is the ethical cop-out I alluded to in section II above. Additionally, as I argued in section I and my discussion of bell hooks' work in the previous chapter, in a culture where certain forms of knowledge and particular subjects' productions of knowledge are deemed objective by default, the pursuit of objectivity inevitably recapitulates hegemonic power relations.

At the more local level of composition studies, the kinds of assessments that are conducted under the reign of objectivity have created disconnects between pedagogy and assessment (Wilson 2008, 47), and even between cherished understandings in composition theory and assessment. The idea of "blind" readings of student writing wrenched from the contexts of the classes in which the texts were composed undermines composition studies' recent emphasis on the rhetor's awareness of audience, as well as the indispensability of the evaluator's knowledge of the particular contexts of any writing occasion. Another problem, as Maja Wilson notes, is that these kinds of assessments leave composition teachers caught in "investing in process for the sake of product" (79). Thus, while the writing process is emphasized in composition pedagogy (and composition theory, despite the rise of postprocess theory), it is often ignored in evaluation protocols geared toward "objective" assessments that are more easily applicable to standardized tests and final products. And, in light of Wilson's explanation of how US rubrics arose from anxiety about the increasing diversification of previously elite university student populations in the nineteenth century (Wilson 2008, chapter 2), one could say there are distressing political implications of objectivity that parallel the obeisance to "facts" I attempted to unsettle in the previous paragraph. Contrary to many compositionists' attempts to create pedagogies of social justice, and to the very belief in objective assessments as a safeguard against prejudice and discrimination, rubrics and related apparatuses of objectivity actually mark the continuing legacy of composition's less laudable gatekeeping functions, in line with Susan Miller's rather unflattering characterization of composition's actual, effected purpose: "to monitor the vernacular writing of the unentitled" (S. Miller 1992, 81).

VII. TOWARD A POSTSTRUCTURALIST COMPOSITION

I conclude this chapter with some questions and speculations on what composition might look like if we took poststructuralism seriously, especially its sustained erosion of the credibility of claims to and valorizations of objectivity. What new kinds of writing might be taught and produced if composition weren't under the sway of objectivity? What new stakes might teachers, students, and others develop in composing and its practices? And what different articulations of grading and writing assessment might have to be developed as a result?

In her critique of ethnography, Trinh points out, "Very few anthropological writings . . . maintain a critical language and even fewer carry within themselves a critique of (their) language" (Trinh 1989, 71). This has changed to some extent in the twenty-five years since Trinh's book was published, with the rise of more self-reflexive and critical work in ethnography and anthropology, as I adumbrate in chapter 5. Certainly, as I suggest in that chapter, composition students' ethnographic projects could be designed to emphasize postcolonial critique and authorial self-referentiality in both content and structure. But what of other kinds of student projects? Could these self-reflexive moves be integrated into other genres as well? For instance, how might students critique the supposed objectivity of research papers within their actual research papers?

In "Grandma's Story," the final chapter of *Woman, Native, Other: Writing Postcoloniality and Feminism,* Trinh offers another model for ethnographic writing, both in terms of her critique of the usual celebration of objectivity and her own writing in this chapter. Her writing interweaves images with personal narrative and theoretical reflection as she unsettles the fact/fiction binary, pointing to the ways in which "stories" reveal "truths": "The truthfulness of the story, as we already know, does not limit itself to the realm of facts" (Trinh 1989, 144). Trinh's work here, the renewed interest in story and personal narrative in composition, and the turn to personal narrative in academic writing in the past few decades—the genesis (in literary theory, anyway) of which is usually traced to Jane Tompkins (1987) highly influential essay "Me and My Shadow"—suggest how hybrid genres might be incorporated into the composition classroom as a way of both interrogating and responding to the monarchy of objectivity.

A return to narrative and story might allow students greater investment in and engagement with writing. A disavowal of the discourse of objectivity might also offer advantages for student composers, who could be encouraged to feel the repudiation of "big" assessment as an opportunity to write for purposes and audiences other than or in addition to grades, teachers, and academic institutions. This may include the self-discovery, self-fulfillment, and commitment to "big" ideas that composition teachers are often wont to flaunt as some of the enduring values and effects of their courses, and some of the practices and dispositions they hope students develop in the process.

Of course, the grading and assessing of writing has never been objective, but to give the lie to the delusion of objectivity means reframing assessment that is currently presented as objective. While denying that assessment is objective might be unsettling for some teachers, students, and administrators (and others outside the university), such a retreat from the large claims of assessment's meaning has the advantage of attaching less weight and power to what are problematic forms of evaluation in the first place. Thus, teaching against objectivity with integrity might also mean that assigning grades and numerical scores to student writing would be too arbitrary to be helpful or meaningful to anyone. Such assessment practices could and should be replaced by others (e.g., prose comments, questions, reader-response), which are less summative and less dependent on the professor/student hierarchies that presume knowledge and expertise flow in one direction only.[10] The end of the monarchy of objectivity can be an unsettling proposition for students, teachers, educational administrators, policymakers, and others, who are accustomed to and comfortable with justifications of authority, pedagogy, and expertise that revolve around assumptions of the objective accumulation, application, and transmission of "knowledge" and learning. However, debunking myths of objectivity would not merely propel more ethical, politically rigorous, and theoretically grounded pedagogy and pedagogical reflection, but would also necessarily focus education on the development of critical consciousness championed by hooks (2000), Freire (2000), and progressive composition teachers and theorists, who have denounced banking models of education.

NOTES

1. See (West 2002, 2, 6) for further discussion of the ways in which "boutique multiculturalism" is bolstered by the "logic of liberal impartiality."
2. For elaboration on liberal pluralism, see Barnard (2005).
3. See, for example, Hayden White's (1975) work on historiography, James Clifford's (1988) revision of ethnography, and work in critical race studies, such as the anthology ed. Richard Delgado (1995). See chapter 5 of this book for further discussion of critiques of ethnography's claims to objectivity.

   Feminist science and feminist critique of science now encompass a large body of scholarship, including influential work by Donna Haraway (1988) and Sandra Harding (1986; 1991). And Thomas Kuhn's (2012) book, *The Structure of Scientific Revolutions*, is now a canonical work in science studies "proper." For further discussion of the critiques of objectivity/universality, see Brodkey (1996, x, 8–9) and Brodkey and Henry (1992).
4. For further discussion of the relationship between "stories" and "truth," see Brodkey (1996) and Trinh (1989, 119ff.).
5. See, for instance, Robinson (2000) for an account of the range of responses to feminism's interrogation of the canon, both by feminists and others. DeJoy issues a parallel warning for composition in her discussion of the difference between inclusion and revision when it comes to feminist challenges to process theory and pedagogy: dominant process models need to revise what it means to teach writing as a process, not

merely accommodate feminist rhetorical traditions within their frameworks (DeJoy 1999, 169–70).

6.   Said's (1993) *Culture and Imperialism* might stand as a representative text here. Said explicitly condemns postmodernism and poststructuralism, and the book evidences Said's allegiance to the literary canon. Said's discussion of the canon takes up the bulk of his massive text, even if the goal is to critique and reread the canon. Said's humanist conceptualization of literature is threaded through the book: "Yet, I do believe that some literature is actually good, and that some is bad, and I remain as conservative as anyone when it comes to, if not the redemptive value of reading a classic rather than staring at a television screen, then the potential enhancement of one's sensibility and consciousness by doing so, by the exercise of one's mind" (319). Despite questioning the notion of objectivity ("reading and writing texts are never neutral activities" (318)), Said's text demonstrates a belief in facts, truth, the "real meanings" of literary texts, and non-partisan scholarship (see, for instance, his pointed distinction between "scholarship" and "struggle" (260)). Additionally, even though Said criticizes imperialist use of the notions of universality and "humanity," he himself incorporates these concepts into his argument: "there is the possibility of a universalism that is not limited or coercive" (229). For further discussion of Said's humanism, see Bové's sympathetic review of *Culture and Imperialism* (Bové 1993).

7.   For some critiques of NCLB and standardized testing, see Anson (2008), Graves (2002), Karp (2008), Kohn (2000), Menken (2008), O'Malley (2008), Peckham (2010), Perelman (2008), Poe (2008), Posnick-Goodwin (2009a; 2009b), Ravitch (2011), Short and Fitzsimmons (2007), and Strauss (2013). See Gilyard (2012) for an overview of resolutions on standardized testing by the the National Council of Teachers of English.

8.   See Menken (2008) for a discussion of the negative impact of standardized testing (including timed essay exams) on English Language Learners, even when they are allowed extra time for tests.

9.   For further discussion of the critique of "scientism," see Phelps (1988, 7ff.).

10.   For further discussion of the problems with grading student writing, and suggestions of alternative models of assessment and feedback, see Tchudi (1997).

8

CONCLUSION
Unbecoming Institutions

Because so many empirical studies of writing are already underway, it's time for someone to undertake a purely theoretical study, one that neither attempts to escape reconditeness nor justifies itself by attempting to emulate social science. Such a study requires the writer to foreground the gaps, dilemmas, and contradictions that all writers encounter when they attempt to insert a new text into the written discourses of the West.

(Jasper Neel 1988, xi)

The preceding chapters have, I hope, offered a sense of the radical challenges to composition business that the upsetting of the six commonplaces—and the values and assumptions on which they rest—offer. Upsetting these commonplaces at least precipitates interrogations of teaching in general, of composition teaching specifically, of student composition, and of commonplace ideas about students as composers. To whom and for whom should students write? Is there anything special about the qualifier "student" in the term "student writer," and, if so, how does and should composition's exceptionalism maintain or explode the tension between "student" and "writer"? What new roles can teachers create for themselves in contingent writing/teaching contexts, where meaning is always in process and interpretation idiosyncratic? And, while we might wish to multiply the possibilities of what the phrase "good writing" may accumulate when "writing" is a verb, does it even make sense any more to speak of "good writing" when "writing" is a noun?

DOI: 10.7330/9780874219470.c008

As I suggested in the conclusions to chapters 3, 5, and 7, hegemonic conceptualizations about grading are thrown into radical indeterminacy in the face of these and other questions that are activated by poststructuralist and postmodern confrontations with conventional assumptions about value, epistemology, hierarchy, subjectivity, agency, and interpretation. Such interrogations may provide additional support to the long tradition of composition scholarship and pedagogy being critical of traditional grading practices (albeit usually for different reasons), and to arguments against grading student writing altogether, if grades are based on the supposed value or correctness of the writing. Under poststructuralism's auspices, audience, purpose, and process may also become less privileged in composition to the extent that the first two injunctions collude with modernist subjectivity and universality as they simultaneously expose composition's incoherence, in concert with postprocess theory's advances on process.[1]

These sheddings might be supplanted by the multiplication of writing (as noun and verb), an acknowledgment that writing (noun and verb) contains and creates many different meanings, and the promotion of play and the possibilities of language in all its indeterminacy. However, they also promise loss: imagined/fear of loss of control; the threat of ignored, diluted, discarded, or even overturned ethical imperatives; and threats of compromising composition's hard-won political exigencies. Nevertheless, as my hedging language suggests, I am not willing to concede any of these losses outright. Certainly some of composition's premises about these precious principles must become more complex—and must change in other ways, too— but multiplication and complication need not trigger nostalgia for clean epistemological lines (and clean disciplinary laundry) and the bankrupt single-issue politics that are their correlative in the public sphere.

Ah, those muddy waters! I have been arguing for the potential value of multiple types of writing, and for refusing to concede a necessary outcome for particular genuses or their specific features. Not either/or, but both, more, and inbetween. I have pushed several competing impulses in this book, both within and across chapters. My urgings of the free play of language after the death of the author (axiom 2) seem to chafe against the demystification of writing that composition has worked so hard to achieve, and against my own critique of romantic constructions of the writer. My skepticism of expressivism might appear at odds with my urging for greater recognition of the unpredictabilities of writing processes and results. And my discomfort with the narrowness of composition's approved forms of writing undermines the poststructuralist skepticism of freedom of form that I rely on to complicate essentialist reclamations or repudiations of theory, action, and genre. My discussion of voice (chapter 4) comes to rest on a fragile tension between, on the one hand, authorial origins and authorial responsibility, and, on the other, the temporal and developmental contingency of language, thought, and processes of composition. Additionally, process' encumbrances sometimes mitigate the reification of one-shot writing brilliance. But in some cases, around any one of these apparent inconsistencies, we need both arguments at once. For the sake of "truth." For the sake of complexity.[2]

Contradiction itself, I would insist, should be left standing. Inconsistency in composition studies might weaken its ongoing claims to scientificity, but perhaps the time has come to fight back against recent and current calls for more empirical and quantitative work in composition, in order to counter narrow and regressive public and political dismissals of and mandates for what the field does and should do. As postprocess and "postpostprocess" theory has urged (e.g., Dobrin, Rice, and Vastola 2011a; Kent 1999), templates of the writing process as predictable, consistent, and repeatable are not only dishonest but also damaging to student writers and rhetoric and composition as a discipline by circumscribing research and pedagogy. If a shift to the local and temporal is in keeping with poststructuralist theory's suspicion of modernist master narratives, ironically, the consistency may lie precisely in the fissures and unpredictabilities—which poststructuralism has theorized so powerfully—of these local scenes. As I suggested in the previous chapter, such a realignment might also help to disturb the onslaught of standardized testing in the United States. And if—in the process of becoming wilder—composition loses some of its supposed functionality, it might be able to ironically capitalize on its putative transdisciplinary cache, not only to intervene at institutional levels to rebut its relegation to a service role but also to muster its institution-wide power to contest the larger corporatization that is exponentially engulfing the US university in the twenty-first century.

The politics of contradiction not only theorize a composition that would better align with the creative arts, with skepticism of positivism and rationalism, and with a radical critique of the scientificity of science, but also complement poststructuralism's distrust of master narratives and denial of unambiguous and unmediated referentiality. To recognize that presence is always/already elusive is neither to give up on politics altogether, nor to concede to uncontextualized relativism or an unfettered individualism that promotes anything goes liberal pluralism. Rather, such a recognition activates an added urgency to the work of language and the sites of language, writing, and discourse in general in order to unfold the complexities of theory as it touches, is touched by, and is composition. Such local unfoldings will speak/write/gesture/link to the politics of location: the location of composition, the locations of authors, the materialities of authors, and the material sites of composition.

NOTES

1. For additional general suggestions of what a poststructuralist composition course might look like, see Schilb (1996, 32) and Neel (1988, xiii).
2. See Hawk (2007) for a thoughtful case for complexity in composition theory, especially in the context of now-rote dismissals of romantic characterizations of the composing process.

APPENDIX

Survey of Composition Faculty at California State University, Northridge

Dear Colleague,

I am doing some research on the role of "intent" in composition classes, and would greatly appreciate it if you would assist me by filling out the brief anonymous survey below, and place your completed survey in my mailbox by 15 November 2009. Feel free to email me if you have any questions or concerns about this survey: ian.barnard@csun.edu.

Thanks so much for your help,

Ian
Ian Barnard

Please answer the following questions about your composition classes by circling the most appropriate answer for each question.

When responding (orally or in writing) to student writing, how important is it to you to establish the student's intention with the piece of writing in order to provide effective feedback?

Very Important   Somewhat important   Not important   Unimportant

---

When students give each other feedback on their paper drafts, how important to giving effective feedback is it that they establish the writer's intention with the paper?

Very Important   Somewhat important   Not important   Unimportant

---

When you discuss professional non-fiction texts (e.g., newspaper articles, essays published in readers) with your students, how important is it to try to figure out the author's intention in writing the piece?

Very Important   Somewhat important   Not important   Unimportant

---

DOI: 10.7330/9780874219470.c009

When you discuss sample student papers with your classes, how important is it to address what the student was trying to achieve in the sample paper under discussion?

Very Important   Somewhat important   Not important   Unimportant

Comments:

REFERENCES

Abercrombie, David. 1963. "Conversation and Spoken Prose." *English Language Teaching* 18 (1): 6–10. http://dx.doi.org/10.1093/elt/XVIII.1.10.

Acker, Kathy. 1990. "Humility: Dead Doll." In *The Seven Cardinal Virtues*, ed. Alison Fell, 112–31. London: Serpent's Tail.

Adler-Kassner, Linda. 2005. *Considering Literacy: Reading and Writing the Educational Experience.* White Plains: Longman.

Adorno, Theodor W. (1948) 1973. *Philosophy of Modern Music.* Translated by Anne G. Mitchell and Wesley W. Blomster. New York: Seabury-Continuum.

Albrecht-Crane, Christa. 2003. "*Whoa*—Theory and Bad Writing." *jac* 23 (4): 857–68.

Alcoff, Linda Martín. 1995. "The Problem of Speaking for Others." In *Who Can Speak?: Authority and Critical Identity*, ed Judith Roof and Robyn Weigman, 97–119. Urbana: University of Illinois Press.

Anderson, Laurie Halse. 1999. *Speak.* New York: Square Fish-Farrar-Macmillan.

Aneja, Anu. 2005. "Of Masks and Masquerades: Performing the Collegial Dance." *symplokē* 13 (1–2): 144–51. http://dx.doi.org/10.1353/sym.2006.0003.

Anker, Susan. 2007. *Real Writing: Paragraphs and Essays for College, Work, and Everyday Life.* 4th ed. Boston: Bedford.

Annas, Pamela J. (1985) 2003. "Style as Politics: A Feminist Approach to the Teaching of Writing." In *Feminism and Composition: A Critical Sourcebook*, ed. Gesa E. Kirsch, Faye Spencer Maor, Lance Massey, Lee Nickoson-Masey, and Mary P. Sheridan-Rabideau, 61–72. Boston: Bedford/St. Martin's.

Anson, Chris M. 2008. "Closed Systems and Standardized Writing Tests." *CCC* 60 (1): 113–28.

Arroyo, Sarah J. 2003. "W/holes: Rethinking Writing Spaces, Moving Toward a Post-Critical Composition." *jac* 23 (2): 259–89.

Baca, Damián. 2008. *Mestiz@ Scripts, Digital Migrations, and the Territories of Writing.* New York: Palgrave Macmillan. http://dx.doi.org/10.1057/9780230612570.

Baecker, Diann. 2007. "'Can You Hear Me Now, Ms. Monster?': Anger, *Thumos*, and First-Year Composition." *Composition Forum* 17. Accessed June 2, 2010. compositionforum.com.

Bakhtin, Mikhail. 1981. *The Dialogic Imagination.* Trans. Caryl Emerson and Michael Holquist. Austin: University of Texas Press.

Barnard, Ian. 1996. "Queerzines and the Fragmentation of Art, Community, Identity, and Politics." *Socialist Review* 26 (1–2): 69–95.

Barnard, Ian. 1998. "Toward a Postmodern Understanding of Separatism." *Women's Studies: An Interdisciplinary Journal* 27 (6): 613–39. http://dx.doi.org/10.1080/00497878.1998.9979235.

Barnard, Ian. 2002. "Whole-Class Workshops: The Transformation of Students Into Writers." *Issues in Writing* 12 (2): 124–43.

Barnard, Ian. 2005. "Civility and Liberal Pluralism." *symplokē* 13 (1–2): 134–43. http://dx.doi.org/10.1353/sym.2006.0005.

DOI: 10.7330/9780874219470.c010

Barnard, Ian. 2009. "Disciplining Queer." *borderlands* 8 (3). Accessed Jan. 10, 2010. borderlands.net.au.

Barnard, Ian. 2010. "The Difficulties of Teaching Non-Western Literature in the United States." *Radical Teacher* 87 (1): 44–54. http://dx.doi.org/10.1353/rdt .0.0078.

Barthes, Roland. (1968) 1998. "The Death of the Author." In *Modern Criticism and Theory: A Reader*, ed. David Lodge, 167–72. New York: Longman.

Bartholomae, David. 1995. "Writing with Teachers: A Conversation with Peter Elbow." *CCC* 46 (1): 62–71.

Bartholomae, David. (1985) 2001. "Inventing the University." In *Literacy: A Critical Sourcebook*, ed. Ellen Cushman, Eugene R. Kintgen, Barry M. Kroll, and Mike Rose, 511–24. Boston: Bedford.

Bawarshi, Anis. 2003. *Genre and the Invention of the Writer: Reconsidering the Place of Invention in Composition*. Logan: Utah State University Press.

Bay, Jennifer. 2002. "The Limits of Argument: A Response to Sean Williams." *jac* 22: 684–97.

Bazerman, Charles. 1997. "The Life of Genre, the Life in the Classroom." In *Genre and Writing: Issues, Arguments, Alternatives*, ed. Wendy Bishop and Hans Ostrom, 19–26. Portsmouth: Boynton/Cook-Heinemann.

Bean, John C, Virginia A. Chappell, and Alice M. Gillam. 2007. *Reading Rhetorically. Brief Edition*. 2nd ed. New York: Pearson-Longman.

Bedford/St. Martin's. 2010. *2010/2011 Catalog for Composition, Developmental English, and Literature Textbooks*. Boston: Bedford.

Belsey, Catherine. 1980. *Critical Practice*. London: Methuen.

Bernard-Donals, Michael. 2008. "Against Publics (Exilic Writing)." *jac* 28 (1–2): 29–54.

Bhabha, Homi. 1988. "The Commitment to Theory." *New Formations* 5: 5–23.

Birkenstein, Cathy. 2010. "We Got the Wrong Gal: Rethinking the 'Bad' Academic Writing of Judith Butler." *College English* 72 (3): 269–83.

Bishop, Wendy. 1999. *Ethnographic Writing Research: Writing it Down, Writing it Up, and Reading it*. Portsmouth: Heinemann-Boynton/Cook.

Bizzell, Patricia. (1982) 2009. "Cognition, Convention, and Certainty: What We Need to Know About Writing." In *The Norton Book of Composition Studies*, ed. Susan Miller, 479–501. New York: Norton.

Blair, Kristine L. 2011. "Review Essay: New Media Affordances and the Connected Life." *CCC* 63 (2): 314–27.

Booth, Wayne C., and Marshall W. Gregory. 1987. *The Harper and Row Rhetoric: Writing as Thinking/Thinking as Writing*. Cambridge: Harper.

Bové, Paul A. 1993. "Hope and Reconciliation: A Review of Edward W. Said." *boundary 2* 20 (2): 266–82. http://dx.doi.org/10.2307/303366.

Bowden, Darsie. 1999. *The Mythology of Voice*. Portsmouth: Boynton/Cook-Heinemann.

Bowden, Darsie. 2003. "Voice." In *Concepts in Composition: Theory and Practice in the Teaching of Writing*, ed. Irene L. Clark, 286–303. Mahwah: Lawrence Erlbaum.

Brady, Laura. 2008. "Retelling the Composition-Literature Story." *College English* 71 (1): 70–81.

Brittenham, Rebecca, and Hildegard Hoeller. 2004. "Voice: The Sight of Sound." In *Key Words for Academic Writers*, by Brittenham and Hoeller, 187–91. New York: Pearson-Longman.

BRITE (brown/white) Ideas! 2005. Toronto.

Brodkey, Linda. 1996. *Writing Permitted in Designated Areas Only.* Minneapolis: University of Minnesota Press.

Brodkey, Linda, and Jim Henry. 1992. "Voice Lessons in a Poststructural Key: Notes on Response and Revision." In *A Rhetoric of Doing: Essays on Written Discourse in Honor of James L. Kinneavy,* ed. Stephen P. Witte, Neil Nakadate, and Roger Cherry, 144–60. Carbondale: Southern Illinois University Press.

Brown, Stephen Gilbert. 2004. "New Writers of the Cultural Sage: The Ethnographic-Self Reconfigured." *jac* 24 (1): 207–27.

Brotzman, Kelly. 2011. "Program Review: Service-Learning in Post-Katrina New Orleans—the Jesuit Way." *Present Tense: A Journal of Rhetoric in Society* 1 (2): 1–7. Accessed May 27, 2013. presenttensejournal.org.

Bryant, Lizbeth. 2005. *Voice as Process.* Portsmouth: Boynton/Cook.

"Building Rubrics." 2009. *Writing @ Case.* Case Western Reserve University. Accessed Aug. 11, 2009. www.case.edu.

Bullock, Richard, Maureen Daly Goggin, and Francine Weinberg. 2010. *The Norton Field Guide to Writing with Readings and Handbook.* 2nd ed. New York: Norton.

Burke, Seán. 2008. *The Death and Return of the Author: Criticism and Subjectivity in Barthes, Foucault and Derrida.* 3rd ed. Edinburgh: Edinburgh University Press.

Burkholder, Elizabeth. 2003. "Andrea's Class at Lanterman High School 2001–2002: A Photo Documentary." PowerPoint slideshow. University of Southern California.

Butler, Judith. 1999. *Gender Trouble: Feminism and the Subversion of Identity.* 10th Anniversary Edition. New York: Routledge.

California State University Task Force on Expository Reading and Writing. 2005. *Expository Reading and Writing Course Semester One.* Version 1.1. Unpublished Binder. The California State University.

Canagarajah, A. Suresh. (2006) 2009. "The Place of World Englishes in Composition: Pluralization Continued." In *The Norton Book of Composition Studies,* ed. Susan Miller, 1617–42. New York: Norton.

Chafe, Wallace, and Deborah Tannen. 1987. "The Relation Between Written and Spoken Language." *Annual Review of Anthropology* 16 (1): 383–407. http://dx.doi.org/10.1146/annurev.an.16.100187.002123.

Chernekoff, Janice. 2003. "Teaching the Rhetorical Possibilities of the Personal Essay." *Composition Forum* 14 (1): 41–47.

Ching, Kory Lawson. 2007. "Theory and its Practice in Composition Studies." *jac* 27 (3–4): 445–69.

Chomsky, Naom. (1966) 1987. "The Responsibility of Intellectuals." In *The Chomsky Reader,* ed. James Peck, 121–36. New York: Pantheon.

Chomsky, Noam. 2005. "Interview by *Thought and Action.*" *Thought and Action* 21: 93–102.

Christian, Barbara. 1987. "The Race for Theory." *Cultural Critique* 6 (6): 51–63. http://dx.doi.org/10.2307/1354255.

The Church of Perpetual Male Bashing: God Help You! 1997. Philadelphia.

Cintron, Ralph. 2002. "The Timidities of Ethnography: A Response to Bruce Horner." *jac* 22 (4): 934–43.

Cliff, Michelle. 2008. "If I Could Write This in Fire, I Would Write This in Fire." In *If I Could Write This in Fire*, by Cliff, 9–32. Minneapolis: University of Minnesota Press.

Clifford, James. 1988. *The Predicament of Culture: Twentieth Century Ethnography, Literature, and Art.* Cambridge, Massachusetts: Harvard University Press.

Clifford, James, and George E. Marcus, eds. 1986. *Writing Culture: The Poetics and Politics of Ethnography.* Berkeley: University of California Press.

Cohen, Patricia. 2011. "Reason Seen More as Weapon Than Path to Truth." *New York Times*, June 14. Accessed June 14, 2011. nytimes.com.

Coles, William E., Jr. 1969. "Freshman Composition: The Circle of Unbelief." *College English* 31 (2): 134–42. http://dx.doi.org/10.2307/374114.

College English 64 (1). 2001. "Special Focus: Personal Writing."

Colomb, Gregory C. 2010. "Franchising the Future." *CCC* 62 (1): 11–30.

Conference on College Composition and Communication. 1974. "Students' Right to Their Own Language." Accessed May 10, 2014. www.ncte.org/cccc/resources/positions/srtolsummary.

Cooper, Marilyn M. 1986. "The Ecology of Writing." *College English* 48 (4): 364–75. http://dx.doi.org/10.2307/377264.

Covino, William A. 1988a. *The Art of Wondering: A Revisionist Return to the History of Rhetoric.* Portsmouth: Heinemann-Boynton/Cook.

Covino, William A. 1988b. "Defining Advanced Composition: Contributions From the History of Rhetoric." *jac* 8 (1–2): 113–22.

Crowley, Sharon. 1987. "Derrida, Deconstruction, and Our Scene of Teaching." *PRE/TEXT* 8 (3–4): 169–83.

Crowley, Sharon. 1994. "A Letter to the Editors." In *Writing Theory and Critical Theory*, ed. John Clifford and John Schilb, 319–26. New York: MLA.

Crowley, Sharon. 1998. *Composition in the University: Historical and Polemical Essays.* Pittsburgh: University of Pittsburgh Press.

Crowley, Sharon. (1985) 2009. "The Evolution of Invention in Current-Traditional Rhetoric: 1850–1970." In *The Norton Book of Composition Studies*, ed. Susan Miller, 333–46. New York: Norton.

Culler, Jonathan, and Kevin Lamb. 2003a. "Introduction: Dressing Up, Dressing Down." In *Just Being Difficult?: Academic Writing in the Public Arena*, ed. Culler and Lamb, 1–12. Palo Alto: Stanford University Press.

Culler, Jonathan, and Kevin Lamb, eds. 2003b. *Just Being Difficult?: Academic Writing in the Public Arena.* Palo Alto: Stanford University Press.

Cushman, Ellen, and Jeffrey T. Grabill. 2008/09. "Writing Theories/Changing Communities: Introduction." *Reflections: A Journal of Public Rhetoric, Civic Writing, and Service Learning* 8 (3): 1–20. Accessed May 26, 2013. reflectionsjournal.net.

Cushman, Ellen, and Erik Green. 2010. "Knowledge Work with the Cherokee Nation: The Pedagogy of Engaging Publics in a Praxis of New Media." In *The Public Work of Rhetoric: Citizen-Scholars and Civic Engagement*, ed. John M. Ackerman and David J. Coogan, 175–92. Columbia: University of South Carolina Press.

Davis, D. Diane. 2000. *Breaking Up (at) Totality: A Rhetoric of Laughter.* Carbondale: Southern Illinois University Press.

DeJoy, Nancy C. 1999. "I Was a Process-Model Baby." In *Post-Process Theory: Beyond the Writing-Process Paradigm*, ed. Thomas Kent, 163–78. Carbondale: Southern Illinois University Press.

Delgado, Richard, ed. 1995. *Critical Race Theory: The Cutting Edge*. Philadelphia: Temple University Press.

Devitt, Amy J. 1993. "Generalizing About Genre: New Conceptions of an Old Concept." *CCC* 44 (4): 573–86.

Dietz, Mary G. 1987. "Context is All: Feminism and Theories of Citizenship." *Daedalus* 116 (4): 1–24.

"Digital Rhetoric." 2013. *CCC* 64 (4): 721.

DPN (Diseased Pariah News). 1990–94. San Francisco.

Dobrin, Sidney I. 2011. *Postcomposition*. Carbondale: Southern Illinois University Press.

Dobrin, Sidney I., J. A. Rice, and Michael Vastola, eds. 2011a. *Beyond Postprocess*. Logan: Utah State University Press.

Dobrin, Sidney I., J. A. Rice, and Michael Vastola. 2011b. "Introduction: A New Postprocess Manifesto: A Plea for Writing." In *Beyond Postprocess*, ed. Dobrin, Rice, and Vastola, 1–18. Logan: Utah State University Press.

Duncombe, Stephen. 1997. *Notes from Underground: Zines and the Politics of Alternative Culture*. New York: Verso.

Ede, Lisa. 1991. "Teaching Writing." In *An Introduction to Composition Studies*, ed. Erika Lindemann and Gary Tate, 118–34. New York: Oxford University Press.

Ede, Lisa, and Andrea Lunsford. 1984. "Audience Addressed/Audience Invoked: The Role of Audience in Composition Theory and Pedagogy." *CCC* 35 (2): 155–71.

Elbow, Peter. 1987. "Closing My Eyes As I Speak: An Argument for Ignoring Audience." *College English* 49 (1): 50–69. http://dx.doi.org/10.2307/377789.

Elbow, Peter. 1994a. "About Voice and Writing." In *Landmark Essays on Voice and Writing*, ed. Elbow, xi–xlvii. Mahwah: Hermagoras-Erlbaum.

Elbow, Peter. 1994b. "What Do We Mean When We Talk about Voice in Texts?" In *Voices on Voice: Perspectives, Definitions, Inquiry*, ed. Kathleen Blake Yancey, 1–35. Urbana: NCTE.

Elbow, Peter. 1995. "Being a Writer vs. Being an Academic." *CCC* 46 (1): 72–83.

English Department Website. 2007. California State University, Northridge. Accessed March 10, 2009. www.csun.edu/english/index.php.

Fabian, Johannes. 1983. *Time and the Other: How Anthropology Makes Its Object*. New York: Columbia University Press.

Faigley, Lester. 1992. *Fragments of Rationality: Postmodernity and the Subject of Composition*. Pittsburgh: University of Pittsburgh Press.

Faigley, Lester. 2012. *The Little Penguin Handbook*. 3rd ed. Boston: Pearson.

Faigley, Lester, Diana George, Anna Palchik, and Cynthia Selfe. 2004. *Picturing Texts*. New York: Norton.

Farr, Marcia. 2003. "Speech Play and Verbal Art: New Perspectives on Feminist Rhetorics." Plenary Address at Fourth Biennial Feminism(s) and Rhetoric(s) Conference, The Ohio State University, Oct. 24.

Fish, Stanley. 1994. *There's No Such Thing as Free Speech and It's a Good Thing, Too*. New York: Oxford University Press.

Fish, Stanley. 2008. *Save the World On Your Own Time*. New York: Oxford University Press.

Fitzgerald, Kelly. 2003. "Homelessness, She Wrote." Unpublished paper. University of Southern California.

Fort, Keith. 1975. "Form, Authority, and the Critical Essay." In *Contemporary Rhetoric*, ed. W. Ross Winterowd, 171–83. New York: Harcourt.

Foucault, Michel. (1969) 1988. "What is an Author?" In *Modern Criticism and Theory: A Reader*, ed. David Lodge, 197–210. New York: Longman.

Franks, Ruth. 2009. "Grading Outline: Research Paper." *Rubrics and Checklists*. The University of Texas at Austin. Accessed Aug. 11, 2009.

Fraser, Nancy. 1996. "Rethinking the Public Sphere: A Contribution to the Critique of Actually Existing Democracy." In *Habermas and the Public Sphere*, ed. Craig Calhoun, 109–42. Cambridge: MIT Press.

Freire, Paulo. (1970) 2000. "The 'Banking' Concept of Education." In *Falling Into Theory: Conflicting Views on Reading Literature*, 2nd ed., ed. David H. Richter, 68–78. Boston: Bedford/St. Martin's.

Freisinger, Randall R. 1994. "Voicing the Self: Toward a Pedagogy of Resistance in a Postmodern Age." In *Voices on Voice: Perspectives, Definitions, Inquiry*, ed. Kathleen Blake Yancey, 242–74. Urbana: NCTE.

Fulkerson, Richard. 2005. "Composition at the Turn of the Twenty-First Century." *CCC* 56 (4): 654–87.

Gearhart, Sally Miller. (1979) 2003. "The Womanization of Rhetoric." In *Feminism and Composition: A Critical Sourcebook*, ed. Gesa E. Kirsch, Faye Spencer Maor, Lance Massey, Lee Nickoson-Masey, and Mary P. Sheridan-Rabideau, 53–60. Boston: Bedford/St. Martin's.

Gee, James Paul. (1999) 2009. "The New Literacy Studies and the 'Social Turn." In *The Norton Book of Composition Studies*, ed. Susan Miller, 1293–310. New York: Norton.

Geertz, Clifford. 1988. *Works and Lives: The Anthropologist as Author*. Stanford: Stanford University Press.

Giltrow, Janet. (2003) 2009. "Legends of the Center: System, Self, and Linguistic Consciousness." In *The Norton Book of Composition Studies*, ed. Susan Miller, 1351–80. New York: Norton.

Gilyard, Keith. 2012. "High Noon for High-Stakes Testing?" *The Council Chronicle* (National Council of Teachers of English), Nov.: 24–25.

Gorzelsky, Gwen. 2009. "Working Boundaries: From Student Resistance to Student Agency." *CCC* 61 (1): 64–84.

Gottschalk, Catherine K. 2011. "Writing From Experience: The Evolving Roles of Personal Writing in a Writing in the Disciplines Program." *Across the Disciplines* 8.1. Accessed June 16, 2011. wac.colostate.edu.

Graff, Gerald. 2003. *Clueless in Academe: How Schooling Obscures the Life of the Mind*. New Haven: Yale University Press.

Graff, Gerald. 2008. "Bringing Writing In From the Cold." *MLA Newsletter* 40 (2): 3–4.

Graff, Gerald, and Cathy Birkenstein. 2010. *"They Say/I Say": The Moves That Matter in Academic Writing*. 2nd ed. New York: Norton.

Graves, Donald. 2002. *Testing is Not Teaching*. Portsmouth: Heinemann.

Greenwald, Glenn. 2012. "Martha Raddatz and the Faux Objectivity of Journalists." *The Guardian*, 12 Oct. Accessed Oct. 14, 2012. http://theguardian.com/.

Haraway, Donna. 1988. "Situated Knowledges: The Science Question in Feminism and the Privilege of Partial Perspective." *Feminist Studies* 14 (3): 575–99.

Harding, Sandra. 1986. *The Science Question in Feminism*. Ithaca: Cornell University Press.

Harding, Sandra. 1991. *Whose Science? Whose Knowledge?: Thinking From Women's Lives*. Ithaca: Cornell University Press.

Harris, Joseph. 2006. *Rewriting: How to Do Things With Texts*. Logan: Utah State University Press.

Harvey, Michael. 2008. *The Nuts and Bolts of College Writing*. Online Companion to the Handbook. Hackett. Accessed March 8, 2009.

Hawk, Byron. 2007. *A Counter-History of Composition: Toward Methodologies of Complexity*. Pittsburgh: University of Pittsburgh Press.

Haynes, Cynthia. 2003. "Writing Offshore: The Disappearing Coastline of Composition Theory." *jac* 23 (4): 667–724.

Heilker, Paul. 2006. "Twenty Years In: An Essay in Two Parts." *CCC* 58 (2): 182–212.

Herrington, Anne, and Marcia Smith Curtis. 2000. *Persons in Process: Four Stories of Writing and Development in College*. Urbana: NCTE.

Hill, Charles. A., and Marguerite Helmers, eds. 2004. *Defining Visual Rhetorics*. Mahwah: Erlbaum.

Himley, Margaret. 2004. "Facing (Up to) 'The Stranger' in Community Service Learning." *CCC* 55 (3): 416–38.

hooks, bell. 1989. "Feminist Theory: A Radical Agenda." In *Talking Back: Thinking Feminist, Thinking Black*, by hooks, 35–41. Boston: South End.

hooks, bell. 1990. "Postmodern Blackness." In *Yearning: Race, Gender, and Cultural Politics*, by hooks, 23–32. Boston: South End.

hooks, bell. 1992. "Madonna: Plantation Mistress or Soul Sister." In *Black Looks: Race and Representation*, by hooks, 157–64. Boston: South End.

hooks, bell. 1994a. "Embracing Change: Teaching in a Multicultural World." In *Teaching to Transgress: Education as the Practice of Freedom*, by hooks, 35–44. New York: Routledge.

hooks, bell. 1994b. *Outlaw Culture: Resisting Representations*. New York: Routledge.

hooks, bell. 1994c. *Teaching to Transgress: Education as the Practice of Freedom*. New York: Routledge.

hooks, bell. 1994d. "'When I Was a Young Soldier for the Revolution': Coming to Voice." In *Landmark Essays on Voice and Writing*, ed. Peter Elbow, 51–58. Mahwah: Hermagoras-Erlbaum.

hooks, bell. (1989) 2000. "Toward a Revolutionary Feminist Pedagogy." In *Falling Into Theory: Conflicting Views on Reading Literature*, ed. David H. Richter, 79–84. 2nd ed. Boston: Bedford/St. Martin's.

Horner, Bruce. 1992. "Rethinking the 'Sociality' of Error: Teaching Editing as Negotiation." *Rhetoric Review* 11 (1): 172–99. http://dx.doi.org/10.1080/07350199209388995.

Horner, Bruce. 1997. "Students, Authorship, and the Work of Composition." *College English* 59 (5): 505–29. http://dx.doi.org/10.2307/378664.

Horner, Bruce. 2000. *Terms of Work for Composition: A Materialist Critique.* Albany: SUNY Press.

Horner, Bruce. 2002. "Critical Ethnography, Ethics, and Work: Rearticulating Labor." *jac* 22 (3): 561–84.

Horner, Bruce, and John Trimbur. 2002. "English Only and US College Composition." *CCC* 53 (4): 594–630.

Horner, Bruce, Min-Zhan Lu, and Paul Kei Matsuda, eds. 2010. *Cross-Language Relations in Composition.* Carbondale: Southern Illinois University Press.

Horvath, Brooke K. (1984) 1994. "The Components of Written Response: A Practical Synthesis of Current Views." In *The Writing Teacher's Sourcebook,* ed. Gary Tate, P. J. Corbett, and Nancy Myers, 207–23. 3rd ed. New York: Oxford University Press.

Howard, Jennifer. 2005. "The Fragmentation of Literary Theory." *The Chronicle of Higher Education,* 16 Dec. Accessed Dec. 13, 2005. chronicle.com.

Howard, Rebecca Moore. 1999. *Standing in the Shadows of Giants: Plagiarists, Authors, Collaborators.* Stamford: Ablex.

Howard, Rebecca Moore. 2006. "The Binaries of Authorship." In *Authorship in Composition Studies,* ed. Tracy Hamler Carrick and Rebecca Moore Howard, 1–12. Boston: Thomson-Wadsworth.

Howard, Rebecca Moore. 2012. "Pedagogical Causes and Rhetorical Consequences of Students' Source Choices." Paper presented at the CCCC annual convention, St. Louis, March 22.

Howard, Rebecca Moore. 2014. *Writing Matters: A Handbook for Writing and Research.* 2nd ed. New York: McGraw-Hill.

Hymes, Dell, ed. (1972) 1999. *Reinventing Anthropology.* Ann Arbor: University of Michigan Press.

Ianetta, Melissa. 2010. "Disciplinarity, Divorce, and the Displacement of Labor Issues: Rereading Histories of Composition and Literature." *CCC* 62 (1): 53–72.

Inoue, Asao B. 2005. "Community-Based Assessment Pedagogy." *Assessing Writing* 9 (3): 208–38. http://dx.doi.org/10.1016/j.asw.2004.12.001.

Inoue, Asao B., and Mya Poe, eds. 2012. *Race and Writing Assessment.* New York: Peter Lang.

Isaacs, Emily, and Phoebe Jackson. 2001. "Introduction: What's the Issue with Student Writing as Public Text?" In *Public Works: Student Writing as Public Text,* ed. Isaacs and Jackson, ix–xix. Portsmouth: Boynton Cook-Heinemann.

Jackson, Brian. 2011. "Neuroscience and the New Urgency of Emotional Appeals." *jac* 31 (3–4): 473–96.

Jarratt, Susan C. (1991) 2003. "Feminism and Composition: The Case for Conflict." In *Feminism and Composition: A Critical Sourcebook,* ed. Gesa E. Kirsch, Faye Spencer Maor, Lance Massey, Lee Nickoson-Masey, and Mary P. Sheridan-Rabideau, 263–80. Boston: Bedford/St. Martin's.

Jarratt, Susan C. (1998) 2009. "Beside Ourselves: Rhetoric and Representation in Postcolonial Feminist Writing." In *The Norton Book of Composition Studies,* ed. Susan Miller, 1381–400. New York: Norton.

Jencks, Christopher, and Meredith Phillips, eds. 1998. *The Black-White Test Score Gap.* Washington: Brookings Institution Press.

Johnson, T. R. 2011. "How Student Writers Develop: Rhetoric, Psychoanalysis, Ethics, Erotics." *jac* 31 (3–4): 533–77.

Jolliffe, David A. 1996. "Argument." In *Keywords in Composition Studies*, ed. Paul Heilker and Peter Vandenberg, 14–7. Portsmouth: Boynton/Cook-Heinemann.

Jolliffe, David A. 2007. "Learning to Read as Continuing Education." *CCC* 58 (3): 470–94.

Jolliffe, David A., and Allison Harl. 2008. "Texts of Our Institutional Lives: Studying the 'Reading Transition' from High School to College: What Are Our Students Reading and Why?" *College English* 70 (6): 599–617.

Kahn, Seth. 2011. "Putting Ethnographic Writing in Context." In *Writing Spaces: Readings on Writing*, Volume 2, ed. Charles Lowe and Pavel Zemliansky, 175–92. Anderson: Parlor. Accessed June 10, 2013. parlorpress.com.

Karp, Stan. 2008. "Contribution to "Forum on Radical Teaching Now." *Radical Teacher* 83:16.

Kastely, James L. 2003. "The Earned Increment: Kenneth Burke's Argument for Inefficiency." *jac* 23 (3): 505–23.

Kennedy, X. J., Dorothy M. Kennedy, and Marcia F. Muth. 2007. *Writing and Revising: A Portable Guide*. 2009 MLA Update. Boston: Bedford.

Kent, Thomas, ed. 1999. *Post-Process Theory: Beyond the Writing Process Paradigm*. Carbondale: Southern Illinois University Press.

Kirklighter, Cristina, Cloe Vincent, and Joseph M. Moxley, eds. 1997. *Voices and Visions: Refiguring Ethnography in Composition*. Portsmouth: Heinemann-Boynton/Cook.

Kirsch, Gesa E., and Peter Mortensen, eds. 1996a. *Ethics and Representation in Qualitative Studies of Literacy*. Urbana: NCTE.

Kirsch, Gesa E., and Peter Mortensen. 1996b. "Introduction: Reflections on Methodology in Literacy Studies." In *Ethics and Representation in Qualitative Studies of Literacy*, ed. Mortensen and Kirsch, xix–xxxiv. Urbana: NCTE.

Klaus, Carl H. 2010. *The Made-Up Self: Impersonation in the Personal Essay*. Iowa City: University of Iowa Press.

Knapp, Steven, and Walter Benn Michaels. (1982) 1985. "Against Theory." In *Against Theory: Literary Studies and the New Pragmatism*, ed. W. J. T. Mitchell, 11–30. Chicago: University of Chicago Press.

Kohn, Alfie. 2000. *The Case Against Standardized Testing: Raising the Scores, Ruining the Schools*. Portsmouth: Heinemann.

Kopelson, Karen. 2008. "Back at the Bar of Utility: Theory and/as Practice in Composition Studies (Reprise)." *jac* 28 (3–4): 587–608.

Koster, Jo, web editor. 2008. "Rubric for Writing/English Courses." Department of English, Winthrop University. Accessed Aug. 11, 2009. Winthrop.edu.

Kuhn, Thomas S. (1962) 2012. *The Structure of Scientific Revolutions*. 50th Anniversary ed. Chicago: University of Chicago Press.

Kutz, Eleanor. 2004. *Exploring Literacy: A Guide to Reading, Writing, and Research*. New York: Pearson-Longman.

Lanham, Richard A. 1983. *Analyzing Prose*. New York: Scribner's.

Lanham, Richard A. (1979) 1987. *Revising Prose*. 2nd ed. New York: Macmillan.

Lanham, Richard A. 2006. *The Economics of Attention: Style and Substance in the Age of Information*. Chicago: University of Chicago Press.

Lanham, Richard A. (1974) 2007. *Style: An Anti-Textbook*. 2nd ed. Philadelphia: Paul Dry.

Lippman, Julie Neff. 2003. "Assessing Writing." In *Concepts in Composition: Theory and Practice in the Teaching of Writing*, ed. Irene L. Clark, 199–220. Mahwah: Erlbaum.

Lu, Min-Zhan. 1994. "Professing Multiculturalism: The Politics of Style in the Contact Zone." *CCC* 45 (4): 442–58.

Lu, Min-Zhan. 2009. "Metaphors Matter: Transcultural Literacy." *jac* 29 (1–2): 285–93.

Lunsford, Andrea A. 1991. "The Nature of Composition Studies." In *An Introduction to Composition Studies*, ed. Erika Lindemann and Gary Tate, 3–14. New York: Oxford University Press.

Lunsford, Andrea, and Lisa Ede. 1990. *Singular Texts/Plural Authors: Perspectives on Collaborative Writing*. Carbondale: Southern Illinois University Press.

Lunsford, Andrea A., and Karen J. Lunsford. 2008. "'Mistakes are a Fact of Life': A National Comparative Study." *CCC* 59 (4): 781–806.

Lunsford, Andrea A., and John J. Ruszkiewicz. 2013. *Everything's an Argument*. 6th ed. Boston: Bedford.

Lunsford, Andrea, Lisa Ede, Beverly Moss, Carole Clark Papper, and Keith Walters. 2013. *Everyone's an Author*. New York: Norton.

Lunsford, Andrea A., Melissa A. Goldthwaite, Gianna M. Marsella, Sandee K. McGlaun, Jennifer Phegley, Rob Stacy, Linda Stingily, and Rebecca Greenberg Taylor. 1996. "Foreword: Considering Research Methods in Composition and Rhetoric." In *Ethics and Representation in Qualitative Studies of Literacy*, ed. Peter Mortensen and Gesa E. Kirsch, vii–xv. Urbana: NCTE.

Lutz, William. 1996. "Textbookspeak." *Curriculum Review* 35 (9): 2.

MacDonald, Susan Peck. 1994. *Professional Academic Writing in the Humanities and Social Sciences*. Carbondale: Southern Illinois University Press.

Marcus, George E., and Michael M. J. Fischer. (1986) 1999. *Anthropology as Cultural Critique: An Experimental Moment in the Human Sciences*. 2nd ed. Chicago: University of Chicago Press.

McLemee, Scott. 2003. "Deconstructing Composition." *The Chronicle of Higher Education*, 21 March. Accessed March 24, 2003. chronicle.com.

McMeniman, Linda. 1999. *From Inquiry to Argument*. Boston: Allyn.

McWhorter, Kathleen T. 2013. *Reflections: Patterns for Reading and Writing*. Boston: Bedford/St. Matin's.

Mead, Margaret. (1928) 2002. *Coming of Age in Samoa*. New York: Perennial-HarperCollins.

Menken, Kate. 2008. *English Learners Left Behind: Standardized Testing as Language Policy*. Clevedon: Multilingual Matters.

Miller, Robert K. 1992. *The Informed Argument: A Multidisciplinary Reader and Guide*. 3rd ed. Fort Worth: Harcourt.

Miller, Susan. 1989. *Rescuing the Subject: A Critical Introduction to Rhetoric and the Writer*. Carbondale: Southern Illinois University Press.

Miller, Susan. 1991. *Textual Carnivals: The Politics of Composition*. Carbondale: Southern Illinois University Press.

Miller, Susan. 1992. "Writing Theory: Theory Writing." In *Methods and Methodology in Composition Research*, ed. Gesa Kirsch and Patricia A. Sullivan, 62–83. Carbondale: Southern Illinois University Press.

Monroe, Barbara. 2009. "Plateau Indian Ways with Words." *CCC* 61 (1): W321–42. Accessed June 16, 2011. ncte.org.

Moore, Cindy. 2005. "Why Feminists Can't Stop Talking About Voice." In *Rhetorical Women: Roles and Representations*, ed. Hildy Miller and Lillian Bridwell-Bowles, 191–205. Tuscaloosa: University of Alabama Press.

Mortimer-Sandilands, Catriona, and Bruce Erickson, eds. 2010. *Queer Ecologies: Sex, Nature, Politics, Desire.* Bloomington: Indiana University Press.

Munday, Judith B. 2008. "Rubric for Written Composition." *HIS Place for Help in School.* Home Educators Association of Virginia. Accessed Aug. 11, 2009.

Murray, Donald M. 1984. *Write to Learn.* Instructor's Edition. 4th ed. Fort Worth: Harcourt.

Murray, Donald. (1972) 2011. "Teach Writing as a Process, Not Product." In *Cross-Talk in Comp Theory*, 2nd ed., ed. Victor Villanueva and Kristin L. Arola, 3–6. Urbana: NCTE.

Naas, Michael. 2003. *Taking on the Tradition: Jacques Derrida and the Legacies of Deconstruction.* Stanford: Stanford University Press.

Nadell, Judith, Linda McMeniman, and John Langan. 2003. *The Longman Writer: Rhetoric, Reader, Handbook.* Instructor's Edition. 5th ed. New York: Longman.

Neel, Jasper. 1988. *Plato, Derrida, and Writing.* Carbondale: Southern Illinois University Press.

Ohmann, Richard. 1976. *English in America: A Radical View of the Profession.* New York: Oxford University Press.

O'Malley, Susan Gushee. 2008. "Contribution to "Forum on Radical Teaching Now." *Radical Teacher* 83: 28.

Objectaphilia 1.1. n.d. San Diego.

Olson, Gary A. 1991. "The Role of Theory in Composition Scholarship." *Freshman English News* 19: 4–5.

Olson, Gary A. 1999. "Toward a Post-Process Composition: Abandoning the Rhetoric of Assertion." In *Post-Process Theory: Beyond the Writing-Process Paradigm*, ed. Thomas Kent, 1–15. Carbondale: Southern Illinois University Press.

Olson, Gary A. 2002. "The Death of Composition as an Intellectual Discipline." In *Rhetoric and Composition as Intellectual Work*, ed. Olson, 23–31. Carbondale: Southern Illinois University Press.

Olson, Gary A. 2008. "Struggling Over Theory, Struggling Over Identity." *jac* 28 (3–4): 583–87.

Olson, Gary A. 2012. Review of *How to Write a Sentence, and How to Read One*, by Stanley Fish. *jac* 32 (1–2): 443–46.

Orr, David W. 1999. "Verbicide." *Conservation Biology* 13 (4): 696–99. http://onlinelibrary.wiley.com/doi/10.1046/j.1523-1739.1999.00004.x/abstract.

Patai, Daphne, and Will H. Corral, eds. 2005. *Theory's Empire: An Anthology of Dissent.* New York: Columbia University Press.

Peckham, Irvin. 2010. "Online Challenge versus Offline ACT." *CCC* 61 (4): 718–45.

Perelman, Les. 2008. "Information Illiteracy and Mass Market Writing Assessments." *CCC* 60 (1): 128–41.

Phelps, Louise Wetherbee. 1988. *Composition as a Human Science: Contributions to the Self-Understanding of a Discipline.* New York: Oxford University Press.

Picabia, Francis. (1920) 2000. "DADA Manifesto." Translated by Margaret I. Lippard. In *Manifesto: A Century of Isms*, ed. Mary Ann Caws, 317–18. Lincoln: University of Nebraska Press.

Poe, Mya. 2008. "Genre, Testing, and the Constructed Realities of Student Achievement." *CCC* 60 (1): 141–52.

Pond, Julia. 2007. "A Moment of Objectivity in the Writing Tutorial." *Writing Lab Newsletter* 32 (3): 7–9. Accessed April 3, 2012. writinglabnewsletter.org.

Porter, James. 2008. Review of *Radical Refusals: Defying Audiences' Expectations*, by John Schilb. *jac* 28 (3–4): 810–16.

Posnick-Goodwin, Sherry. 2009a. "In the Age of Testing, Can Schools Teach Critical Thinking?" *California Educator* 13 (9): 8–16.

Posnick-Goodwin, Sherry. 2009b. "What is a Test Score?" *California Educator* 14 (3): 8–11.

Posnick-Goodwin, Sherry. 2009c. "The Write Stuff." *California Educator* 14 (4). Accessed December 31, 2009. cta.org.

Poster, Carol. 1998. "(Re)positioning Pedagogy: A Feminist Historiography of Aristotle's *Rhetorica*." In *Feminist Interpretations of Aristotle*, ed. Cynthia A. Freeland, 327–50. University Park: Penn State University Press.

Pounds, Wayne. 1987. "Agents and Actions: An Excursion in Plain Style." *Rhetoric Review* 6 (1): 94–106. http://dx.doi.org/10.1080/07350198709359156.

Powell, Malea. 2012. "2012 CCCC Chair's Address: Stories Take Place: A Performance in One Act." *CCC* 64 (2): 383–406.

Powers, Anne. 2010. "A Pop Music Critic Takes on Wagner's 'Ring' Cycle. First Up: 'Das Rheingold.'" *The Los Angeles Times*, June 9. Accessed June 9, 2010. latimes.com.

Pringle, Ian. 1983. "Why Teach Style? A Review-Essay." *CCC* 34: 91–98.

Purcell-Gates, Victoria. (1997) 2001. "A World Without Print." In *Literacy: A Critical Sourcebook*, ed. Ellen Cushman, Eugene R. Kintgen, Barry M. Kroll, and Mike Rose, 402–17. New York: Bedford.

Rage Against the University! 2006. Toronto.

Rallin, Aneil, and Ian Barnard. 2008. "The Politics of Persuasion versus the Construction of Alternative Communities: Zines in the Writing Classroom." *Reflections: A Journal of Writing, Service-Learning, and Community Literacy* 7 (3). Accessed June 29, 2012. reflectionsjournal.net.

Ramage, John D., John C. Bean, and June Johnson. 2003. *The Allyn and Bacon Guide to Writing*. 3rd ed. New York: Longman.

Ravitch, Diane. 2011. "Let Your Voice Be Heard: A Q & A with Academic Historian Diane Ravitch." Interviewed by Mary Ellen Flannery. *Thought and Action* 27. Accessed June 15, 2012. nea.org.

Remley, Dirk. 2012. "Reconsidering the Range of Reciprocity in Community-Based Research and Service Learning: You Don't Have to be an Activist to Give Back." *Community Literacy Journal* 6 (2): 115–32. http://dx.doi.org/10 .1353/clj.2012.0025.

Rice, Jeff. 2005. "The New Media Instructor: Cultural Capital and Writing Instruction." In *Don't Call it That: The Composition Practicum*, ed. Sidney I. Dobrin, 266–83. Urbana: NCTE.

Ringgold, Matthew. 2011. "Facebook Status." Unpublished Moodle post. California State University, Northridge.

Roberts-Miller, Patricia. 2002. "Fighting Without Hatred: Hannah Arendt's Agonistic Rhetoric." *jac* 22 (3): 585–601.

Robillard, Amy E. 2006a. "Students and Authors in Composition Scholarship." In *Authorship in Composition Studies,* ed. Tracy Hamler Carrick and Rebecca Moore Howard, 41–74. Boston: Thomson-Wadsworth.

Robillard, Amy E. 2006b. "*Young Scholars* Affecting Composition: A Challenge to Disciplinary Citation Practices." *College English* 68 (3): 253–70. http://dx.doi.org/10.2307/25472151.

Robinson, Lillian S. (1983) 2000. "Reason Our Text: Feminist Challenges to the Literary Canon." In *Falling Into Theory: Conflicting Views on Reading Literature,* 2nd ed., ed. David H. Richter, 153–66. Boston: Bedford/St. Martin's.

Roen, Duane, Gregory R. Glau, and Barry M. Maid. 2013. *The McGraw-Hill Guide: Writing for College, Writing for Life.* 3rd ed. New York: McGraw-Hill.

Rollins, Brooke. 2006. "Inheriting Deconstruction: Rhetoric and Composition's Missed Encounter with Jacques Derrida." *College English* 69 (1): 11–29. http://dx.doi.org/10.2307/25472186.

Romano, Tom. 2004. *Crafting Authentic Voice.* Portsmouth: Heinemann.

Rooney, Ellen. 1989. *Seductive Reasoning: Pluralism as the Problematic of Contemporary Literary Theory.* Ithaca: Cornell University Press.

Roskelly, Hephzibah, and David A. Jolliffe. 2008. *Everyday Use: Rhetoric at Work in Reading and Writing.* 2nd ed. White Plains: Pearson Longman.

Rottenberg, Annette T., and Donna Haisty Winchell. 2012. *Elements of Argument: A Text and Reader.* 10th ed. Boston: Bedford.

Royster, Jacqueline Jones. 1996. "When the First Voice You Hear is Not Your Own." *CCC* 47 (1): 29–40.

Rumsey, Suzanna Kesler, and Tanja Nihiser. 2011. "Expectation, Reality, and Rectification: The Merits of Failed Service Learning." *Community Literacy Journal* 5 (2): 135–51.

Said, Edward. (1978) 1979. *Orientalism.* New York: Vintage-Random.

Said, Edward. 1989. "Representing the Colonized: Anthropology's Interlocutors." *Critical Inquiry* 15: 205–25.

Said, Edward. 1993. *Culture and Imperialism.* New York: Knopf.

Salvatori, Mariolina R., and Patricia A. Donahue. 2004. *The Elements (and Pleasures) of Difficulty.* New York: Pearson-Longman.

"Sample Grading Rubrics." 2006. Florida State University. Accessed August 11, 2009. writing.fsu.edu.

Sánchez, Raúl. 2005. *The Function of Theory in Composition Studies.* Albany: State University of New York Press.

Schilb, John. 1996. *Between the Lines: Relating Composition Theory and Literary Theory.* Portsmouth: Boynton Cook-Heinemann.

Schilb, John. 2007. *Rhetorical Refusals: Defying Audiences' Expectations.* Carbondale: Southern Illinois University Press.

Sebranek, Patrick, Verne Meyer, and Dave Kemper. 1996. *Writers Inc: A Student Handbook for Writing and Learning.* Wilmington: Great Source Education Group-Houghton.

Selfe, Cynthia. 2009. "The Movement of Air, The Breath of Meaning: Aurality and Multimodal Composing." *CCC* 60 (4): 616–63.

Sharpton, Al. 2012. "Politics Nation." MSNBC, May 31.

Sheridan, Mary P. 2012. "Making Ethnography Our Own: Why and How Writing Studies Must Redefine Core Research Practices." In *Writing Studies Research in Practice: Methods and Methodologies*, ed. Lee Nickoson and Mary P. Sheridan, 73–85. Carbondale: Southern Illinois University Press.

Shoar, Michael. 2011. "Facebook." Unpublished Moodle post. California State University, Northridge.

Short, Deborah J, and Shannon Fitzsimmons. 2007. *Double the Work: Challenges and Solutions to Acquiring Language and Academic Literacy for Adolescent English Language Learners*. A Report to Carnegie Corporation of New York. Washington, DC: Alliance for Excellent Education. Accessed June 15, 2012. all4ed.org.

Skwire, Sarah E., and David Skwire. 2005. *Writing With a Thesis: A Rhetoric and Reader*. 9th ed. Boston: Wadsworth.

Smith, Daniel. 2003. "Ethics and 'Bad Writing': Dialectics, Reading, and Affective Pedagogy." *jac* 23 (3): 525–52.

Smitherman, Geneva. 1977. *Talkin' and Testifyin': The Language of Black America*. Detroit: Wayne State University Press.

Solanas, Valerie. (1968) 1991. *Scum Manifesto*. London: Phoenix.

Spayde, Jon. 2004. "We'll Always Have Paris: French Theory is Dead. Long May It Live." *Utne Reader*, November–December: 76–77.

Spellmeyer, Kurt. 1993. *Common Ground: Dialogue, Understanding, and the Teaching of Composition*. Englewood Cliffs: Prentice Hall.

Spigelman, Candace. 2004. *Personally Speaking: Experience as Evidence in Academic Discourse*. Carbondale: Southern Illinois University Press.

Strauss, Valerie. 2013. "A Warning to College Profs From a High School Teacher." *Washington Post*, Feb. 9. Accessed Aug. 10, 2013. washingtonpost.com.

Sunstein, Bonnie Stone, and Elizabeth Chiseri-Strater. 2012. *FieldWorking: Reading and Writing Research*. 4th ed. Boston: Bedford.

Tannen, Deborah. 1982. "Oral and Literate Strategies in Spoken and Written Narratives." *Language* 58 (1): 1–21. http://dx.doi.org/10.2307/413530.

Tchudi, Stephen, ed. 1997. *Alternatives to Grading Student Writing*. Urbana: NCTE.

Tompkins, Jane. 1987. "Me and My Shadow." *New Literary History* 19 (1): 169–78. http://dx.doi.org/10.2307/469310.

Trimble, Thomas. 2008/09. "Into the Field: The Use of Student-Authored Ethnography in Service-Learning Settings." *Reflections: A Journal of Public Rhetoric, Civic Writing, and Service Learning* 8 (3): 52–75. Accessed May 26, 2013. reflectionsjournal.net.

Trimbur, John. 1999. "The Problem of Freshman English (Only): Toward Programs of Study in Writing." *WPA: Writing Program Administration* 22 (3): 9–30. Accessed June 19, 2012. wpacouncil.org.

Trinh T. Minh-ha, dir. 1982. *Reassemblage*. Second Decade Films, Inc.

Trinh T. Minh-ha. 1985. "Interview with Trinh T. Minh-ha." Interviewed by Constance Penley and Andrew Ross. *Camera Obscura* 13–14: 87–103.

Trinh T. Minh-ha. 1989. *Woman, Native, Other: Writing Postcoloniality and Feminism*. Bloomington: Indiana University Press.

Trinh T. Minh-ha. 1997. "Not You/Like You: Postcolonial Women and the Interlocking Questions of Identity and Difference." In *Dangerous Liaisons:*

Gender, Nation, and Postcolonial Perspectives, ed. Anne McClintock, Aamir Mufti, and Ella Shohat, 415–19. Minneapolis: University of Minnesota Press.

Ulmer, Gregory L. 2003. *Internet Invention: From Literacy to Electracy.* New York: Longman.

Vandenberg, Peter. 1996. "Voice." In *Keywords in Composition Studies,* ed. Paul Heilker and Peter Vandenberg, 236–9. Portsmouth: Boynton/Cook-Heinemann.

Vidali, Amy. 2011. "Embodying/Disabling Plagiarism." *jac* 31 (3–4): 752–69. Print.

Villanueva, Victor. 2009. "Maybe a Colony: And Still Another Critique of the Comp Community." In *The Norton Book of Composition Studies,* ed. Susan Miller, 991–8. New York: Norton.

Vitanza, Victor. 1991. "Three Countertheses: Or, A Critical In(ter)vention into Composition Theories and Pedagogies." In *Contending With Words: Composition and Rhetoric in a Postmodern Age,* ed. Patricia Harkin and John Schilb, 139–72. New York: MLA.

Wampole, Christy. 2013. "The Essayification of Everything." *The New York Times,* May 26. Accessed June 2, 2013. nytimes.com.

Wan, Amy J. 1999. "Not Just for Kids Anymore: Using Zines in the Classroom." *Radical Teacher* 55: 15–9.

We Like Poo 1 (3). n.d. San Francisco.

Weathers, Winston. 1980. *An Alternate Style: Options in Composition.* Rochelle Park: Hayden.

Weisser, Christian R. 2008. "Subaltern Couterpublics and the Discourse of Protest." *jac* 28 (3–4): 608–20.

Welch, Nancy. 2002. " 'And Now That I Know Them': Composing Mutuality in a Service Learning Course." *CCC* 54 (2): 243–63.

Wells, Susan. 2003. "Just Difficult Enough: Writers' Desires and Readers' Economies." *jac* 23 (3): 487–503.

West, Thomas R. 2002. *Signs of Struggle: The Rhetorical Politics of Cultural Difference.* Albany: SUNY Press.

White, Hayden. 1975. *Metahistory: The Historical Imagination in Nineteenth-Century Europe.* Baltimore: Johns Hopkins University Press.

Wiederhold, Eve. 2008. "Feminist Rhetoric and Representational Fatigue." *jac* 28 (1–2): 123–49.

Williams, Bronwyn T. 2010. "Seeking New Worlds: The Study of Writing Beyond Our Classrooms." *CCC* 62 (1): 127–46.

Williams, Joseph M. 1981. "The Phenomenology of Error." *CCC* 32 (2): 152–68.

Williams, Joseph M., Gregory G. Colomb, Jonathan D'Errico, and Karen Tracey. 2003. *The Craft of Argument with Readings.* New York: Longman.

Williams, Raymond. 1980. "Ideas of Nature." *Problems in Materialism and Culture: Selected Essays,* by Williams, 67–85. London: Verso.

Wilson, Maja. 2008. *Rethinking Rubrics in Writing Assessment.* Portsmouth: Heinemann.

Wimsatt, William K., and Monroe C. Beardsley. (1946) 1989. "The Intentional Fallacy." In *The Critical Tradition: Classic Texts and Contemporary Trends,* ed. David H. Richter, 1383–91. New York: Bedford.

Winterowd, W. Ross. 1994. "Rediscovering the Essay." In *Composition Theory for the Postmodern Classroom,* ed. Gary A. Olson and Sidney I. Dobrin, 121–31. Albany: SUNY Press.

Worsham, Lynn. 1991. "Writing Against Writing: The Predicament of *Écriture Féminine* in Composition Studies." In *Contending With Words: Composition and Rhetoric in a Postmodern Age*, ed. Patricia Harkin and John Schilb, 82–104. New York: MLA.

Worsham, Lynn. 2002. "Coming to Terms: Theory, Writing, Politics." In *Rhetoric and Composition as Intellectual Work*, ed. Gary A. Olson, 101–14. Carbondale: Southern Illinois University Press.

"Writing Improves When Publishing is the Goal." 2006. *The Council Chronicle* 15 (3): 2–3.

Wysocki, Anne Francis, Johndon Johnson-Eilola, Cynthia L. Selfe, and Geoffrey Sirc, eds. 2004. *Writing New Media: Theory and Applications for Expanding the Teaching of Composition*. Logan: Utah State University Press.

Yagoda, Ben. 2004. "Style: A Pleasure for the Reader, or the Writer?" *The Chronicle of Higher Education*, 13 August. Accessed August 10, 2004. chronicle.com.

Yancey, Kathleen Blake. 1994a. "Introduction: Definition, Intersection, and Difference—Mapping the Landscape of Voice." In *Voices on Voice: Perspectives, Definitions, Inquiry*, ed. Yancey, vii–xxiv. Urbana: NCTE.

Yancey, Kathleen Blake, ed. 1994b. *Voices on Voice: Perspectives, Definitions, Inquiry*. Urbana: NCTE.

Young, Vershawn Ashanti. 2009. "'Nah, We Straight': An Argument Against Code Switching." *jac* 29 (1–2): 49–76.

Zavarzadeh, Mas'ud, and Donald Morton. 1986–87. "Theory, Pedagogy, Politics: The Crisis of 'The Subject' in the Humanities." *boundary 2* 15 (1–2): 1–22.

Zebroski, James Thomas. 2011. "Critical Theory, Critical Pedagogy, and the Reconceptualization of Rhetoric and Composition." *jac* 31 (1–2): 283–307.

Zeiger, William. 1985. "The Exploratory Essay: Enfranchising the Spirit of Inquiry in College Composition." *College English* 47 (5): 454–66. http://dx.doi.org/10.2307/376877.

Zwagerman, Sean. 2009. Review of *Pluralizing Plagiarism: Identities, Contexts, Pedagogies*, ed. Rebecca Moore Howard and Amy E. Robillard. *jac* 29 (4): 882–90.

ABOUT THE AUTHOR

IAN BARNARD is an associate professor of rhetoric and composition at Chapman University. He previously taught for ten years at California State University, Northridge, where he served as chair of the University Writing Council and coordinator of Stretch Composition in the Department of English. Barnard is the author of *Queer Race: Cultural Interventions in the Racial Politics of Queer Theory* and articles and book chapters on composition, queer theory, South African literature and culture, and pedagogy. He lives in Los Angeles.

INDEX